MY VISION OF

Against a backdrop of the familiar r
pleasures of rally driving, the compa
Lynda Cantor's daily round was like many others; things done for fun, things done because that was how they should be. And then it started to change: in matter-of-fact words, Lynda writes of a darkening world, of curious moments of apparent clumsiness, of a curtain slowly being drawn to shut out all light.

If Lynda had merely coped with what was happening to her alone, she would have deserved admiration and emulation. But she reached out, researching into this thing that had dared to try to imprison her, and in doing so discovered a community of families and individuals struggling to understand and live with Retinitis Pigmentosa. What was to be done? Why, create an organisation dedicated to funding scientific research into the condition. Wouldn't anybody do the same? Well, no. But she would. And has done.

Lynda took her own experience, and moulded it into making things happen for the good of generations still to come, of people affected by this wretched pathology. She lifted her own life in the process, and thousands could one day know her as the agent by which their own lives were transformed.

Lord Mark Birdwood
Member BRPS Board of Trustees

To

With best wishes

Lynda Card.

and

Yvonne Higgins

MY VISION OF HOPE

A Remarkable Story

Lynda Cantor

with

Yvonne Higgins

Lynda Cantor

Published 2006 by
LYNDA CANTOR

PO Box 350, Buckingham MK18 1GZ
www.brps.org.uk

Printed 2006 by
Buckingham Colour Press
1 Osier Way
Swan Business Park
Buckingham MK18 1TB
Tel: 01280 824000
www.buckinghamcolour.com

Copyright © LYNDA CANTOR 2006

No part of this publication may be reproduced by any
means whatsoever without the prior permission of the author

ISBN
0-9552575-0-6
978-0-9552575-0-6

Cover design: Iona Stern
Cover photograph of Lynda and Laddie: John Credland
Proofreader: Sylvia Welling

Proceeds from the sale of this book are in aid of the Medical Research Fund
of the British Retinitis Pigmentosa Society – Fighting Blindness

I dedicate this book to the memory of my aunt,
Dr Jessie Mole.

Also to my beloved Guide Dog,
Laddie
who, at the age of six, sadly died from cancer
as this book went to print.

I would like to thank **Yvonne Higgins** wholeheartedly for being by my side helping to write this book. The project would never have happened without her assistance, steadfast encouragement and confident optimism.

Yvonne is a retired teacher of the deaf and has a nephew with Usher Syndrome. She has supported the work of the British Retinitis Pigmentosa Society for many years.

ACKNOWLEDGEMENTS

I would like to thank those who took a keen interest in reading parts or the whole draft of this book for their helpful and stimulating comments: Lord Mark Birdwood, David Cantor, Judith Marshall, Mary McSparron, Alison Rampling, Sir Alan and Lady Rudge, Hilary and Geoffrey Strutt.

I am indebted to Selwyn Higgins for writing the Report on the Medical Research Progress. Also to Professors John Marshall and Robin Ali for checking the medical references in the book, and for their amendments to the medical section and the glossary. My sincere thanks to each of them.

I have been fortunate in having Iona Stern to design the cover of the book and do other related artwork. Likewise in having Sylvia Welling to proofread the book. Their professional skills have enhanced the book and I am grateful to them both.

The dedicated members of staff at the BRPS office Kate Samwell, Paul Netherton, Margaret Williams and Vivienne Eldridge have assisted me in various ways. I would like to express my appreciation to them all and in particular to Vivienne Eldridge for the laborious task of typing the manuscript. In addition I wish to thank those who have contributed photographs.

Finally I have valued the support and encouragement given to me during the writing of this book by my friends and fellow workers in the fight against RP. My heartfelt thanks to them all.

FOREWORD

Retinitis Pigmentosa is a wasting disease of the eye, incurable and in most cases resulting in a relentless progression toward total blindness. To be diagnosed with RP even in today's more enlightened times comes as a paralysing shock, not only to the sufferer, but also to their family and friends. How much worse it must have been for Lynda Cantor thirty years ago when, as a young and newly separated mother with two young children, she was informed that this was to be her lot.

Faced with such a sentence, many would have sunk into despair, or at least focused themselves solely upon their own problems. But that was not Lynda's way and beginning with a card index on her dining room table she started down the long hard road that led to the founding and growth of the British Retinitis Pigmentosa Society. Today the BRPS, a nationwide charity, plays an important role in a worldwide network of charities, dedicated to fighting blindness by raising and applying funds for medical research into RP, and providing welfare and mutual support to sufferers.

With courage, humour and resilience, Lynda has turned personal adversity into public good. Here then are her memoirs of how it was done. This is a memorable record of the determination and hard work of Lynda and of her colleagues and helpers who played their part, both in building the Society and in its subsequent achievements. An inspirational story, told with good humour by its central player.

Sir Alan Rudge
Chairman BRPS Board of Trustees

CONTENTS

PROLOGUE		xi
1.	THE BEGINNINGS	1
	Stumbling Along	
2.	A SOCIETY IS BORN	8
	A First Time for Everything	
3.	TREATMENTS	15
	So-Called	
4.	FINDING THE WAY	22
	The Problem of Mobility	
5.	GRASS ROOTS	40
	The Importance of Branches	
6.	MONEY, MONEY, MONEY	50
	Fundraising and Grants	
7.	SPREADING THE WORD	73
	The Need for Publicity	
8.	IT'S THAT TIME OF YEAR AGAIN	86
	The AGM – A Few Memories	
9.	HELPING HANDS	98
	An Office, a Board of Trustees and a Management Committee	
10.	WHO WILL LISTEN?	113
	Welfare and the Helpline	
11.	BEYOND THESE SHORES	125
	Retina International	
12.	FIGHTING BLINDNESS	140
	Members Help Research	
13.	EUPHORIA ON THE MOUNTAIN TOPS	148
	Highlights for the Society	
EPILOGUE		164
APPENDICES:		
	1. A Report on the Medical Research Progress to date by Selwyn Higgins	165
	2. The Medical and Scientific Advisory Board for the BRPS	173
GLOSSARY		176

Words marked with an asterisk (*) throughout the book are defined in the glossary.

PROLOGUE

This is a story of amazing coincidences, personal encounters, dogged determination and selfless commitment by countless numbers of people who have worked tirelessly for the British Retinitis Pigmentosa Society (BRPS): Fighting Blindness.

All these threads come together both in the extensive programme of medical research into Retinitis Pigmentosa (RP) and the support given to RP sufferers through the Helpline, meetings and publications. The threads run as themes throughout the chapters of this book forming a rich tapestry: colourful, complex and continuous.

I have written neither my autobiography nor a chronological history of BRPS. Each chapter gives a glimpse into one aspect of the Society's work and is based upon my memoirs. Over the past thirty years I have met so many people dedicated to the work of BRPS it would be impossible to write about them all. Whether or not they are named they have contributed to this testimony of triumph in the face of adversity.

Retinitis Pigmentosa (pigmentation of the retina) is the name given to a group of hereditary diseases of the retina, which is the light-sensitive tissue in the back of the eye, in which the first stages of seeing take place. With RP, the retina slowly loses its ability to transmit pictures to the brain. Often the first symptom is night blindness, followed by narrowing side vision, leading to what is sometimes called tunnel vision and in some cases total blindness. In related conditions the loss can begin in the central area and spread outwards, causing early loss of detail vision. Some people with RP have other related problems, one example being Usher Syndrome* where RP is combined with hearing loss.

RP is a progressive disease for which there is, at present, no cure or treatment that will halt its progress.

Whom does it affect?

RP can affect anyone who has inherited the faulty gene* and the symptoms may occur at any age. Usually they become apparent in young adults but often children and sometimes babies are affected. RP is the greatest untreatable cause of hereditary sight loss amongst people of working age.

How does it occur?

RP is inherited by one of three modes of transmission and these are explained in detail in the BRPS booklet 'Genetics and RP'.

What is BRPS doing to help?

The British Retinitis Pigmentosa Society, Fighting Blindness is the only British charity dedicated to finding a cure for Retinitis Pigmentosa. It was formed in 1975 by a small group of people with RP, and some interested friends. Since then it has grown to 3,000 members with over 30 Branches around the UK. In thirty years, its members have raised over £7 million, which has funded 185 research projects.

By funding research, BRPS intends to find a cure for RP, whilst giving support and guidance to its members and their families along the way. BRPS is a founder member of Retina International.

Chapter 1

THE BEGINNINGS
Stumbling Along

*"I wandered lonely as a cloud
That floats on high o'er vales and hills ..."*
The Daffodils. William Wordsworth 1770-1850

A small girl, perhaps eight years old, stood watching a lady tapping her way along the pavement with a white cane. The child stared bewildered and frightened. That scene remained vivid in her memory for a long time.

I was that child, on holiday in Aberdeen with my grandmother and the lady was one of my great aunts. Little did I realise then that more than fifty years later I would be using a white cane to find my way around the park while my Guide Dog was having a free run.

My children were quite young. Helen was about four years old and Anthony almost two when I noticed I started to trip over things they had left on the floor, bump into half open doors, miss kerbs and steps. I even walked into some scaffolding one morning. Nor could I manage so well in the dark. I had always hated the dark, switching on the light the moment daylight began to fade. As a child I was terrified of the dark, insisting the landing light was left on all night, and a night-light left on in the bedroom. If I awoke and the room was in complete darkness I could not see a thing. No chink of light below the curtains, no dark shapes of the furniture comforted me. Fear would consume me.

I dismissed all this until one day I was reversing my car out of the driveway and backed straight into my neighbour's car. Why hadn't I seen it? It was parked in the right place, perfectly visible, leaving me plenty of space. I decided I must need glasses. My doctor, who also happened to be a personal friend, could see nothing wrong with my eyes but suggested I visit an optician.

As the optician examined my eyes he became quiet. This set me wondering. Eventually he said, "I would like you to see an ophthalmologist*. I don't think I can help you."

My doctor arranged for me to go to Moorfields Eye Hospital in London. Even then I didn't think there was anything seriously wrong with my eyes.

The day of the appointment arrived. It was February 1971. Nobody had warned me what to expect. I drove to Moorfields from my home in Surrey taking the children and my au pair girl with me, as she could drive – how useful that proved to be later in the afternoon. By the time I had been given a series of eye drops, test upon test and three hours had passed I knew something was badly wrong.

My anxiety had grown with each test. First I had been given a visual field test to find out how much side vision I had. This had taken almost thirty minutes to test each eye. I sat in a darkened room with my chin resting on the machine. I had to look straight at the spot in the centre of the machine and press the buzzer every time a light spot appeared on the screen. The colour test was less daunting. I was simply asked to state the colour of the balls as I saw them on the screen.

The ERG (electroretinogram) and EOG (electroculogram) tests were more complex. After sitting in a dark room for twenty minutes eye drops and contact lenses, attached by wires to the machine, were put in each eye. For the ERG I watched white flashing lights on the screen. The technician recorded the results, which revealed the amount of light the retina at the back of my eyes was transmitting to my brain. This took approximately thirty minutes. The EOG took another thirty minutes to complete. Wires or electrodes were taped to my skin near my eyes and one to my forehead. I was asked to move my eyes from right to left between two lights, once a minute for fifteen minutes with the room lights off and then for fifteen minutes with the lights on. This measured the electrical charge from the back to the front of my eyes.

The final test was to take pictures of the back of my eyes by Fundus Photography. A fluorescein dye was injected into my arm. This caused my skin to become a deep bright yellow for up to four hours, but it meant that my retinas and their blood vessels could be studied in more detail. Again I had to rest my chin on a machine while first one eye was photographed and then the other.

"Does this mean I am going blind?" I asked the consultant when the tests were finished.

"You have an inherited eye disease called Retinitis Pigmentosa and in some cases it does lead to total blindness," came the answer. "I will send a full report to your own doctor." When I visited my GP later, he knew little about the condition.

The journey home, from Moorfields, was dreamlike. I could not believe what I had been told. The eye drops and after effects of the tests still blurred my vision. We reached home and put the children to bed, by that time my vision was clearing. I went to see Mary, a great friend who lived nearby. As soon as I walked into her kitchen she exclaimed, "Whatever's the matter with you?"

"On top of everything else I'm going to lose my eyesight," I replied. The words were out. But still I felt the truth was unreal. We talked and talked, finally deciding that I should get a second opinion.

Anyway the first thing I had to practise was saying Retinitis Pigmentosa, because I found that quite a mouthful. I then spent a long time discovering who specialised in the disease. This led me to ophthalmologists* Tom Casey, Barrie Jay and Trevor Roper. Each one told me the same:

"I don't know how long it will take."

"You may not go completely blind."

"You ought to prepare yourself."

I went into complete denial, resolving to forget about it. I studied my eyes in the mirror. They looked quite normal to me. They weren't diseased. I could read the telephone directory, watch television programmes and see to carry out most household chores. I would just have to be careful in the dark and make sure I didn't fall over the children's toys.

Much later I learnt that an early symptom of RP is night blindness, a condition in which the eyes of a person with RP cannot adjust to the dark, as do healthy eyes. As the disease progresses there is a loss of peripheral vision so that objects immediately below, above and to the sides are not seen. I always think it must be like looking through two cardboard tubes similar to those inside toilet rolls.

For two years it was put to the back of my mind, as much as you can put something like that to the back of the mind. I took the children on holiday. I went by myself on a wonderful trip to Hong Kong, and while I was there I saw an ophthalmologist. Once again my diagnosis was confirmed.

On returning to the UK I had many things to do. I suppose subconsciously I was thinking, "Just in case …". I felt the best thing to do for my children was to have their names put down for boarding schools. If I was not able to drive in the future I didn't want them to miss out. At boarding school they could join in all the activities young people do if they have a sighted parent who could drive them everywhere.

In 1969 I had been admitted to hospital for an operation on my leg. It was a small clinic, which we nicknamed 'Pitt's Palace' as a Mr Pitt was the surgeon. There were only eight beds, each in a private room. In one of these private rooms was an American girl called Susie, who had gangrene of the hand. Neither of us felt ill and found being confined to hospital boring. We therefore spent a lot of time in each other's company and after we were discharged from hospital we took our children swimming together. Our friendship grew and on returning to America some years later she thought of me when she saw an advertisement in the 'New York Times'.

She sent me a newspaper cutting from the 'New York Times', which had been printed on 18th November 1973, my birthday. It was a whole page of Broadsheet advertising the recently formed American RP Foundation for patients with Retinitis Pigmentosa. She telephoned me saying she thought the best thing I could do was to go over to the States. She would get an appointment for me to see Dr Eliot Berson, an ophthalmologist* at the Massachusetts Ear and Eye clinic in Boston. Later he became director of the Berman-Gund laboratory for the study of Retinal Degeneration*.

In great haste I prepared for a trip to America. I was absolutely convinced the Americans would be able to cure me. Full of optimism Susie took me to the Massachusetts Ear & Eye Clinic where I was examined and given exactly the same tests as I had at Moorfields. The prognosis was just as bad. In fact my eyes had deteriorated and so it was even worse. Eliot Berson told me that in all probability I would become totally blind. He gave me a prescription for hideous dark glasses and suggested I contact someone called Ben Berman who had founded and was running the National Retinitis Pigmentosa Foundation in America. He had three daughters, two of whom were diagnosed with RP after one had fallen down an uncovered manhole.

I could not extend my visit, so I spoke to Ben Berman on the telephone. He sent me the names and addresses of a number of people in the UK who had written to him suggesting I contact them with the idea of forming a similar Foundation in the UK. I filed the letter away and put it out of my mind.

My husband had left me in November 1970, three months before my first appointment at Moorfields. He could not believe that there was anything wrong with my eyes. He regarded it as emotional blackmail on my part. We were divorced in July 1972.

I had been told that RP was an inherited disease. Where had it come from in my family? I was an only child, and my mother had no living relatives. My father had one sister, Jessie, who never married. Their mother was one of four sisters and although one of them lost her sight, her blindness was not caused by RP according to her medical records. However, she suffered from cataracts*, which can be associated with RP. My parents were divorced when I was eight years old and as they had no further contact with each other I had grown up knowing little of our family history. It has been assumed, therefore, that my RP must be the recessive* type. This means that despite my parents not having RP both were carriers of the faulty gene, giving a one in four possibility of their child developing the condition.

I have often wondered what it would be like to be part of a large family. Yet I have a family of friends, which grew in ever widening circles with the formation of BRPS.

NB **Words marked with an asterisk (*) throughout the book are defined in the glossary.**

Chapter 2

A SOCIETY IS BORN
A First Time for Everything

"... mighty things from small beginnings grow."
John Dryden 1631-1700

I took the plunge one evening. I would write to those people Ben Berman had told me about. After all, I would be interested to know how they coped with the progressive loss of their eyesight. The children were asleep in bed. Out came my electric typewriter and I wrote to all the names and addresses Ben Berman had given me. It took me quite a long time. Finally when I had completed the task and there was a neat little pile of envelopes on the table, I vaguely wondered what the outcome would be.

To my amazement within two or three days I had my first reply. A letter from a lady called Mary Guest. I had thought all the people I had written to were RP sufferers. Not so. Mary told me she was a teacher of the deaf, teaching a deaf young person and she could not understand why he had been knocked down by a motor car while crossing the road. She talked to his parents and suggested he should have an eye test. He was diagnosed with Retinitis Pigmentosa. Both the parents and Mary Guest were stunned. What was this condition? They had never heard of it. The ophthalmologist* told them it was very rare.

A few months later Mary accompanied her husband on a business trip to America. She was watching the television one evening, with her two young sons, when there flashed on the screen: 'Help to save sight. Contact the National Retinitis Pigmentosa Foundation (NRPF).'

Mary was astonished. She scribbled down the address and wrote to Ben Berman. He sent her a lot of information, which included a statement that the combination of deafness and loss of eyesight is called Usher Syndrome*. In order to keep abreast of information Mary joined the Californian Chapter or Branch of the American RP Foundation.

The next reply to my letter was from a young man called Alan Wells. His brother Keith, who was totally blind with RP, worked for Barclays Bank. Alan was keen to help form a charity. "Hang on," I thought, "this has gone from a little club to a charity!"

My third letter was from Dennis Fuller, who had a wife, a daughter and a son, all suffering from Usher Syndrome*. As he lived in Cumbria he was unable to come and see me, but later I travelled up to meet him.

Eric Katz OBE then answered my letter. He lived n Epsom where I had spent most of my childhood. Eric also had RP and suggested he paid me a visit.

James Hudson also wrote to me. He was American and a novelist, married to a French girl, Claudia. They lived in London with their two young sons. He too had RP and was eager that we should meet.

Another reply came from a social worker with RP, Humphrey Stevenson. He wasn't so keen to meet, but asked me to let him know the outcome of any meeting I arranged.

At this point I felt I needed some help. My father's sister, Jessie Mole, who became known simply as Aunt Jessie within BRPS for a long time, was also my Godmother. She had begun her career as one of the first research chemists for ICI. Later she moved to the field of atomic energy research. For many years she was the scientific administrator of a department at the Atomic Energy Research Centre in Harwell, and wrote their annual report for the Government.

I spent an unforgettable weekend with her. On a warm spring day in the garden of her house in Sunningwell, just outside Oxford, sipping coffee under an apple tree I told my aunt about these people who had written back to me.

"I'm going to start a charity," I said thoughtfully. "We could raise money. We might even raise enough for some research. We might raise enough for all the research needed to find a cure." My enthusiasm was carrying me away. My aunt chuckled. She was a wise woman.

"Do you know how to run a meeting with an agenda?" she enquired.

"Nooo," said I.

"You will have to learn about committee meetings," she remarked.

That sounded boring. But by the time I left that Sunday evening she and I knew that this was a very good idea. She would assist me in any way she could.

It was obvious that a meeting had to be organised, but where in London could we hold such a meeting? I didn't know anywhere. I was explaining this over dinner one night, to some friends.

"I'll give you a hand," said the husband. "Just for the first meeting, you understand, so you can get to know each other."

This was a kind offer from Kenny Wellings. He had stood for Parliament as a Liberal candidate and could arrange for us to use a room at the Liberal Club for our first meeting. This was good, but things were to become even better. A letter arrived from Ben Berman in America saying that Professor Alan Laties, head of their medical research team, was visiting London. He felt sure that Alan would be willing to meet, help, and advise us in any way he could if we so wished. This was just what we needed. We now had a meeting place and a medical advisor to speak to us.

Somehow we managed to find a date when everyone was free to come: Mary Guest, Dennis Fuller, Jimmy Hudson, Alan Wells, Alan Laties and myself.

This was the first committee meeting I had ever attended. It was April 1975. There were so many decisions to make. We needed headed notepaper for example. More importantly how could we pass on the knowledge we had acquired to fellow sufferers? I felt strongly that one of my greatest needs, as a patient, had been an overwhelming desire for information. If only someone could have given me a booklet, or a leaflet explaining the genetic inheritance* and what was wrong with my eyesight. Why was a faulty gene causing my sight to deteriorate? We concluded we could go no further without a medical advisory board.

"I know," I said brightly, "I will contact all the ophthalmologists* I've seen."

"How many have you seen?" they gasped.

"Five or six," I replied. I did not tell them that utter despair had compelled me to consult one after another in a desperate attempt to find help. I went home to type a letter to all the ophthalmologists I had consulted about my own eyesight.

I was overjoyed when by return of post a letter came from Tom Casey saying he would be delighted to serve on a medical advisory board. This was the encouragement I needed. Full of pride I telephoned Aunt Jessie.

"I really think I ought to come and help you," she stated. "It's going to be big."

"Don't be silly," I expostulated. "It's a rare eye disease. Only a small number of people are involved."

I wrote to Ben Berman telling him how enthusiastic people were, talking about starting a charity. My aunt urged me to find someone within London University medical research team to help me.

"How do I do that?" I demanded.

"I have a friend from my student days at Bedford College, London University, Harry Carlisle. He is now a professor at Birkbeck College in the department of Crystallography* at the University," she replied.

We went along to see him, had tea and I explained I wanted to find out if anyone was doing medical research into this eye disease in the UK. Would it be possible for him to introduce me to someone at the Institute of Ophthalmology*?

"That's easy," came the answer. "I have contacts at the Institute and will enquire if anyone is working on or has any interest in RP and would be willing to meet you."

Dr John Marshall responded. He had some interest in the colony of albino rats (known as Royal College of Surgeons or 'RCS' rats) that develop a form of RP. He felt he should meet me to tell me that I was wasting my time. During the meeting he tried to hand me a piece of paper. As it came to my side I did not see it immediately. He realised at once that I had RP. He told me that it would cost millions of pounds to fund such research. I simply said, "OK, we'll raise it." He agreed to attend our next meeting and went away to formulate a research policy for RP. I had found a research worker and he had found someone with RP.

My committee was growing. My aunt had joined and I had persuaded Professor Harry Carlisle to be chairman. Mary Guest, Alan Wells, Jimmy Hudson were already members. Now John Marshall was coming.

For more than thirty years John has been our constant mentor, becoming chairman of our Medical Advisory Panel and a member of the Board of Trustees. He has given his time and expertise unstintingly, sharing in all the major decisions of the Society.

Meanwhile, on the other side of the Atlantic, Ben Berman had heard of our developments. He wrote to the BBC 'In Touch' programme, informing them I had started a charity for RP sufferers and their families. It was not long before I was contacted by Jane Finnis who was a presenter of the programme. She asked me if I would be willing to go on the programme to explain what I was hoping to achieve. My response was immediate.

"On the radio! You are joking. No way. I can't even pronounce Retinitis Pigmentosa properly." However, she persuaded me to do the interview.

Never, in my wildest dreams, did I envisage the response there would be to that programme. Letters came flooding in, about 500 in all. It was obvious I needed some secretarial help. Which of my girlfriends could touch-type at speed? I found one, but with two small children her time was limited.

Another outcome of the broadcast was a telephone call from the office of a local newspaper, 'The Surrey Mirror'. They had heard about the broadcast and would like to send a reporter to interview me. Not only had I done my first broadcast I was now going to give my first interview with the Press. It was one of the best articles a reporter has written about our work. The facts were correct and he ended with my words, "Find me a millionaire so that we can make it work."

Two days later when the newspaper was published, the telephone rang. It was the newspaper's office. A volunteer, who had worked at the Leatherhead School for the Blind, had telephoned offering his services to help. Might they give him my telephone number? So arrived Eric Tucker. He was marvellous and helped me answer all those letters.

I knew I must not lose the names and addresses of any of those people who had written to me. I devised a system. Every time we replied to a letter I wrote out an index card with their name, address and date when they had contacted us. This became the starting-point for our present membership database. Eric and I spent evening after evening around the dining room table working away.

At the same time my Aunt Jessie was busily suggesting what we should be doing to launch a charity. Membership forms were needed. Should we have a membership subscription? Who would meet the cost of stationery and stamps? Events were galloping along.

In due course it became apparent that we would have to apply to the Charity Commissioners to become a registered charity. We would have to choose a name and open a bank account among other things. I learnt so much in that first year. It took more than eighteen months for our application to the Charity Commissioners to be successful. My Aunt Jessie wrote the Deed of Trust and was responsible for all the correspondence to the Charity Commissioners.

At last on the 6th June 1976 the BRPS was registered as Charity Number 271729.

Chapter 3

TREATMENTS
So-Called

"He that is strucken blind cannot forget
The precious treasure of his eyesight lost."
Romeo and Juliet. William Shakespeare 1564-1616

Three popular melodies droned away in the back of my mind. I found myself humming them as I went about my daily chores.

"Um!" I reflected. "They remind me of these so-called treatments."

'From Russia with Love', the catchy theme tune of that film, for the Russian treatment.

'The Flight of the Bumble Bee', for the bee sting treatment.

'Edelweiss', for the so-called Swiss treatment.

There was continuous coverage of these alleged treatments for RP in the Press. Why this coverage was given to RP sufferers seeking treatment remains a mystery. It may be because RP was incurable and involves the loss of eyesight. Certainly, it was emotional. Moreover, vast amounts of money were raised to enable people with RP to undergo such treatment.

The first treatment I heard of was the Russian treatment. Appearing on the front page of 'The Times' newspaper, about a year before we started the Society, was a photograph of a pretty little girl with her mother. She was going blind from Retinitis Pigmentosa. Her family had heard through Trade Union newspapers that in Russia people were being treated for this rare eye disease. They managed to raise the large sum of money required for a visit to the Helmholtz Eye Clinic in Moscow. A particular ophthalmologist working at this Clinic was practising the 'treatment'. The little girl underwent a series of injections called Encad extracted from yeast RNA.

While she was there I received a picture postcard one morning from my friend Stephanie, who was in Moscow. I had met Stephanie in Sorrento two years earlier when I was on holiday with the children. We had spent many evenings together chatting after the children had gone to bed. She spoke fluent Russian. To my surprise I learnt from her postcard that she was in Moscow as an interpreter for the mother of this little girl, who was being treated for the same rare eye disease as mine.

Along with many other people my hopes were raised when I first heard of this possible treatment. It was not long, however, before doubts and fears crept into my mind. Some three years later, the controversy was still raging. I telephoned John Marshall, wrote to Barrie Jay and contacted the other ophthalmologists* I had seen. They all said the same, "The claims associated with this treatment are not confirmed by organised clinical trials."

"The scientific rationale behind it is theoretical and unconvincing."

They told me there was a great deal of criticism from other centres in Russia. Moreover, representatives of the British and American ophthalmic fraternities had attended a meeting held in Moscow, and they were in no way convinced by the Russian claims presented at the meeting, that there were any permanent benefits from the treatment.

At about the same time a long article was published in the colour supplement of the 'Observer' newspaper about Jack Warner, who appeared in the television series 'Dixon of Dock Green'. He was having his arthritis treated by a lady called Julia whose unorthodox treatment involved stinging people with bees.

The article stated she also cured people who had the inherited eye disease Retinitis Pigmentosa.

Numerous patients endeavoured to undergo this treatment. I met many of them, but there was one particular case that I will always remember.

One evening I received a telephone call at home, from a school teacher. He was looking after two children who had flown in from Australia with their father. The father had to return to Australia because his wife was dying of cancer. The school teacher proceeded to tell me about this extraordinary woman who was trying to cure the children's eye disease by stinging them with bees. He was enraged. He said it was nothing but a false way of making money and the children were in a great deal of pain. He told me he was going to get this woman exposed. He wrote to the television programme 'Watchdog'. In time they took up the case and eventually they did expose her. Sadly this did not deter a number of patients who continued to seek her treatment.

Another patient, Andy Potok, was an American and a member of the Human Sciences Committee for the American RP Foundation. He was Polish by birth. His parents had escaped from the Second World War by going to live in America. He had one uncle who lived in London and when his eyesight began to deteriorate he decided to try out the bee sting treatment. As an artist he was desperate to save his sight. When I first met him he had been living in London for at least three months, undergoing the bee sting treatment two or three times a week. Initially he concealed the fact that he was having this treatment. However as we got to know each other he described the treatment in detail. It was bizarre. In addition to the bee stings, sugar in any form, in any food was banned. Instead Julia's honey only was to be used. She sold this at a high price. Alcohol was completely denied, although the bees were given whisky to drink! After six months of this treatment Andy was so ill he quit and returned to the States. He did, however, write a book about his experience of the treatment. Gradually less and less was heard about it.

The third treatment was offered by Professor Bangerter at his private Opus Clinic in St Gallen, Switzerland. Once again huge sums of money were raised to help people seeking this treatment. I spoke to Professor Gloor at Basle University. He asked me not to refer to this therapy as 'the Swiss treatment', because it was not supported by other ophthalmologists* in Switzerland. I met several patients who described to me what had happened when taking this treatment. Their eyes were anaesthetised and an amniotic membrane of a chicken's egg was implanted beneath the thin membrane covering their eyes. They told me Professor Bangerter also gave them a course of pleoptics, which are exercises of the eye to help patients to use as much as possible of their remaining visual acuity*. I knew only too well that any orthoptic clinic* could provide such a course.

The controversy over these so-called treatments was widespread and constant. They were featured on the Radio 4 news programme 'Today', on numerous news bulletins and on the front pages of newspapers with headlines such as 'CHILD GOING BLIND WILL BE SAVED BY TREATMENT IN SWITZERLAND'.

We continually issued Press statements informing people these treatments could not produce the outcome everyone desired so much. I did not know one patient who had experienced any improvement whatsoever in their eyesight.

After consulting the Society's medical advisors I wrote to all the editors of the National Press, Radio and Television news programmes expressing our concerns regarding these treatments. However, in retrospect, I realise that had it not been for these so-called treatments the Society would never have had such extensive and ongoing publicity.

At one stage the publicity given to the Russian treatment was raging as headlines in so many newspapers that the Institute of Ophthalmology* gave a Press Conference on 2nd June 1976. I was asked to represent a patient organisation. John Marshall, Alan Bird, Barrie Jay, Geoffrey Arden were all interviewed. Later they all became members of our Medical Advisory Board. For the first time I appeared on the BBC Nine O'clock evening news, as it was in those days, and John Marshall was interviewed on the 'Jimmy Young Show'.

There were three television news programmes in 1978. One of our Press statements had fallen into the hands of Austen Mitchell, the Labour MP for Grimsby. His wife, Linda McDougall, was a producer for the ITV programme 'World in Action'. She decided to do a thirty minute documentary about the treatment in Switzerland. I arranged for her to meet John Marshall. He put all the medical facts to her, showing that this treatment could not possibly work. She flew out to Switzerland, to St Gallen, and filmed the Opus Clinic as eight members of one family arrived from Liverpool. All eight were seeking treatment.

The television programme 'Pebble Mill at One' interviewed me together with the mother and her daughter who had undergone the Russian treatment, in an attempt by the programme producers to present both points of view. It was a distressing experience.

Another interview was for the programme which followed the BBC Six O'clock evening news. By this time I had my first Guide Dog, Yasmin. The BBC sent a taxi for us. We both travelled up to London in style. I walked through the Blue Peter studio, which was dark and quiet. I couldn't see very much in the dark, of course, and there were countless cables coiled over the floor. The poor dog couldn't guide me and I nearly tripped flat on my face. We entered the appointed studio. The presenter was broadcasting, sitting at a low, glass table with two white chairs, neither of which I was able to see clearly. I was expected to climb a step, avoid falling over the glass table and sit down in the chair beside him under the glare of blazing lights. Bright light, whether it is from the sun or artificial lighting dazzles those with RP. I froze, saying there was no way I could manage this. Gallantly the presenter came to help me while a film clip was being shown. He settled me with my Guide Dog lying at my feet and, after another film clip of the Helmholtz Clinic, interviewed me. During a news item following our interview he thanked me and reached down behind his chair for his glass, but Yasmin had found it first.

He laughed and a few days later I received a cheque with a note, "This is for your new charity and not to be spent on whisky for your Guide Dog."

Years later another so-called treatment was offered by Dr Palaez in Cuba. This too received a great deal of publicity. It involved the use of electro-stimulation, ozone and eye surgery. Eventually Dr Palaez agreed to meet the scientific advisors of IRPA (The International RP Association) in June 1991. As a result they felt they could not recommend or endorse Dr Palaez's experimental treatments. There was no known medical or scientific basis for it. No acceptable data had been published showing that this attempted treatment was effective in treating RP. Particularly worrying was the lack of any information about the surgery. It would be irresponsible, therefore, to expect an ophthalmologist to take care of a patient after an operation of which he had no knowledge. In fact in some instances it was thought the procedures might be harmful.

Soon after this our medical advisors led by Professor Alan Bird decided it was necessary to update the Society's official guide to treatments. How invaluable this was when as recently as 2003 our members were targeted with letters advertising the treatment offered by Dr Palaez.

Throughout the past one hundred years there have been fifty apparent cures for Retinitis Pigmentosa. However, none has stood the test of time.

Chapter 4

FINDING THE WAY
The Problem of Mobility

"Go placidly amid the noise and haste."
Max Ehrmann 1872-1945

"Come back in two years' time," the consultant at Moorfields Eye Hospital had told me at the end of my first visit in 1971. They would need to run further tests, which would indicate any deterioration in my eyesight. I was sure my central vision had remained good. I could sew the name tabs on my children's school clothes. I could still do my tapestry and other needlework. I could see colours very clearly. I wasn't so sure about my peripheral vision. Sometimes I would sit in the garden and focusing my eyes on a tree I would note all I could see to the sides, above and below without moving my eyes or my head. I knew these were primitive tests. I tried not to do them, thinking it was best to leave it to the professionals.

I waited in some trepidation. The appointment card came from Moorfields, as I knew it would. This time I decided to go by public transport accompanied by my friend, Mary. I was given two of the tests I'd had before. I sat facing my consultant after they were over.

"Well?" I asked.

It must be difficult to tell someone their eyesight is failing.

Gently he replied, "There is some deterioration. I would like you to go on the partially sighted register."

"What does that mean?" I asked in alarm.

"It means the Social Services will be aware of your failing eyesight. Someone will come to see you to find out if they can advise or help you in any way."

A month later a visitor arrived from Social Services and asked me a lot of questions.

"Would you like mobility lessons?"

She produced two white canes. One was a symbol cane to show people I had poor eyesight. It was lightweight and 85 cms long. The other was a long cane, which measured 122 cms in length. By swinging it from side to side along the ground in front of me I would be able to locate obstacles. Social Services would provide training to use this long cane.

"Would you like to learn Braille?" "Would you like to be put in touch with the Surrey Voluntary Association for the Blind?"

I was in a state of shock. Dazed, I felt I was entering a new world I knew nothing about. After my visitor left I looked at the two canes.

"What shall I do with them?" I wondered.

The symbol cane was a neat little job. It folded into four. The long cane was different. A long, stiff rod, nearly as high as me. It came up to my shoulder.

I said to myself firmly, "I'll put that in the cupboard."

In due course I did receive mobility training, but I was neither good at it nor did I like it. I knew I was making life difficult for myself by resisting it. I decided to practise. When I went to meetings or up to London I slid the little symbol cane into my handbag, thinking at least I could get it out if I became really worried or anxious. For many months it remained tucked away in my handbag.

One day the telephone rang. A cheerful voice at the other end announced,

"I am the secretary of the Surrey Voluntary Association for the

Blind. I was wondering if you needed anything?"

I resisted the temptation to say, "Some new eyes please."

He was very understanding and said that any time I needed anything I was to contact him. He began sending me their Newsletter.

I struggled on, not wanting to use even the symbol cane. Crossing the road, going up and down steps in a strange environment was becoming increasingly difficult. I stopped going out unless accompanied by a friend. The children didn't like me using a cane either. They would say, "Mummy, we can hold your hand. We can cross the road together. We can go around the supermarket together. Don't worry."

Shortly after being diagnosed with Retinitis Pigmentosa I gave up driving voluntarily. I knew I still had useful central vision, but it was difficult to assess my peripheral vision. Also there was the problem of dazzling lights, as well as not being able to see in the dark. I realised, too, that no insurance company would cover me in the event of an accident if I drove knowing I was visually impaired and had not declared it both to them and the DVLA. I considered all these aspects and came to the conclusion I had to stop driving.

It was one of the hardest decisions I have ever made. My former husband had been a car rally driver. I had joined in all the excitement of it; preparing the pace notes and accompanying the back-up crew we had to take with us. We competed in the RAC Rally of Great Britain, the Scottish and Irish Rallies, the Tulip Rally in Holland and the Portuguese Rally. We met many famous drivers. We had driven two Mini Coopers followed by a twin cam Ford Escort. Cars, driving, mechanical repairs, racing events had dominated our lives for three years.

Nonetheless I knew the time had come to cease driving. I felt it was morally wrong to drive, being aware I had something wrong with my eyesight. How could I live with the knowledge if I killed or maimed somebody? Not being able to drive would create problems for me, of course. I was a single parent living some distance from the children's schools, in a small village in the heart of Surrey.

"People will help out," encouraged friends. And they did.

A cable from my American friend, Susie, brought the sad news that tragically her husband had died quite suddenly and unexpectedly. They were living in Hong Kong at the time, but as soon as she had sorted out her affairs she would be coming to the UK to visit her children in boarding schools. We agreed that she should live with me for a while. In the school holidays her children also stayed when they were not visiting relatives in America. They were happy times with four children, a dog and a hamster. We were so busy there was no time to dwell on my loss of sight. Something was always happening. Susie, of course, took over all the driving. It was marvellous. I didn't feel so isolated.

After two years Susie thought she should take her children back to America to live where they would have all the members of their extended family around them. Naturally I was disappointed, but I would have to stand on my own two feet sooner or later.

I arranged to have another attempt at learning to use the long cane. I knew my eyesight had deteriorated further and I asked for an appointment to see my consultant at Moorfields Eye Hospital again. Living with me Susie had noticed it too. Little things. I did not walk so quickly. I was not so confident around the house. You accommodate your sight deterioration without realising it. My central vision was still good however.

September 1976 marked another stage. I went back to Moorfields and this time was put on the blind register. You are placed on the blind register if you have lost a certain number of degrees for both your central and peripheral vision. By now I only had approximately 6 degrees of central vision whereas a person with good eyesight has 139 degrees to 154 degrees. The tunnel was becoming very small. In a strange way it was a relief. I had arrived, I was registered blind. I had got to get on and adjust to it. I must learn all the skills I could to help myself and my family.

What could I do? The long cane still made me feel uncomfortable, despite further training with it. Nor did I really like the symbol cane. I decided to apply for a Guide Dog. We had always owned a pet dog ever since my daughter Helen was three months old. She was a Labrador called Pippa and was very much part of the family. I love dogs and had always had a dog, wherever I lived. The decision to have a dog therefore was not difficult, and if it had the added bonus of being my eyes it would give me my freedom again. I would be able to go out when I wanted. Perhaps I would regain my independence. My hopes were high.

———◆———

Guide Dogs for the Blind are usually bred at the Association's Breeding Centre, Tollgate. When they are six weeks old they go to live with a volunteer puppy walker for a year. They are house trained and taught to go to the toilet by the commands 'Spend' and 'Get Busy'. They are taken to supermarkets, pubs, churches, libraries and shops. They are taken to visit families where there are children, dogs or cats. They are taken in cars, on buses and trains. Gradually they become accustomed to all these situations.

After a year the puppy goes to one of the centres of the Guide Dogs for the Blind Association (GDBA) to begin training in harness. It is trained over obstacle courses of various widths, to stop at kerbs and to locate zebra crossings. All this takes approximately six to eight months. The instructor will then visit the blind person at home in order to select the most suitable dog for that person's needs.

An instructor arrived to see me. After discussing the type of routes I would need to do with a Guide Dog we went out for a walk, the instructor leading the way. My neighbours must have thought it very peculiar. There was Lynda being led on the end of a harness by a strange man. Explanations soon put their minds at rest. I was to have a Guide Dog.

The GDBA wrote to tell me I was on their waiting list. As soon as they found a suitable dog they would contact me. Much to my joy this did not take long as I was called for training in November 1977.

Once more my birthday became a milestone. After a very busy day in Birmingham with our Midlands Branch, I went straight from that meeting to the Wokingham Guide Dog Centre to begin training with my first Guide Dog. This residential course would last for four weeks.

In those days the GDBA had centres all around the country and you went to the one nearest your home. Wokingham was a purpose-built one storey building accommodating up to twelve students, as we were called. Then, of course, there were the kennels for 120 to 150 dogs, all in different stages of training. I was very apprehensive. I did not know what to expect. While I was familiarising myself with my bedroom there was a knock on my door and David Griffiths introduced himself as the instructor who had trained my dog. He took me to the lounge where I met the other students before starting to learn my way around the house.

That first day, a Saturday, we were taught the different positions for our feet when going down a kerb and turning left or right. It was important to master these foot positions for a dog to guide smoothly. We were given the dog's harness, its play collar which had bells on it so that it could be heard when running free, its check collar and lead. There seemed a lot to learn.

At last on Sunday morning after breakfast we all returned to our rooms to await the arrival of our own dog. In the bedroom was a large dog bed. From this moment the dog would not leave me. I sat waiting, listening intently to the sound of paws padding along the corridor, dogs panting and check chains clinking. A knock came on my door. There was my instructor with Yasmin. She was a golden Labrador/retriever cross bitch. She was small for her breed, weighing only 58lbs or just over 26 kilograms. She was very pleased to see me. "This is a good start," I thought. After a few minutes David left us. Yasmin went to the door and whined pitifully. I had been told that these dogs become very attached to their instructor, and it was important in those first weeks that you bond with your dog, weaning her away from her instructor. I found it quite taxing. Every time David walked into the lounge Yasmin was on her feet, tail wagging in greeting.

To begin with we stayed in the house, taking our dogs everywhere with us. We were allowed to take them into the lounge, but had to make the dog lie down at the side of our chair. We were taught the routine for feeding the dog. She must 'Sit' and 'Wait.' She was not allowed to touch the food until I gave her the command. I had to teach her to 'Stay' in her own bed. Yasmin was keen on my bed and not so keen on hers. I soon remedied that. All this was part of learning to control the dog. Some dogs were better behaved than others and in the evenings we shared many hilarious stories about the antics of our dogs.

When the time came for us to start working the dogs in harness we were taken to the obstacle course in the grounds. Yasmin had to gauge the width and height I needed to walk safely under, along or around the obstacles. The first occasion we allowed the dogs to have a free run on the enclosed big grassy areas we had to replace the check lead with the play collar and make the dog 'Sit' before she could go for a run. I was given a whistle to use after I had called her back by name. Hopefully she would come straight back, which I rewarded with a treat. We could take our dog for a free run whenever we liked.

I woke early on the day I was going to walk alone with my dog for the first time. It was nerve-racking. However, I soon learnt and I knew my instructor was nearby. I didn't realise where exactly. Sometimes he was on a bicycle following me, and at other times he walked discreetly behind. The concentration was intense. I retired to bed each night utterly exhausted.

As the training progressed we were taken out in the minibus to do longer and more difficult walks. We were given directions to remember.

"Walk straight ahead along the road. Two down kerbs (which means cross two side roads or drives). Turn left. After four down kerbs turn left again."

The walks were usually in blocks. The Guide Dogs didn't know the routes. They had to obey our instructions. The only commands they knew were 'Forward', 'Back', 'Left', 'Right', 'Sit', and 'Stay'. Until the dog knows the route it can only follow your instructions if you are in a strange place, therefore you need directions in order to give the dog the correct command.

It was really scary when we were taken into the crowded town centre of Reading. However, my confidence grew each day as I crossed busy roads. To reinforce Yasmin's awareness of danger from approaching traffic my instructor would appear unexpectedly in his car.

Meanwhile a growing backlog of letters concerning the Society's matters waited to be answered. I asked the Controller of the Centre if I might use the quiet room during the daily free periods for some of my BRPS correspondence.

Priscilla, who helped me with the secretarial work at home, arrived with a suitcase full of records, files, headed writing paper, envelopes and stamps. Laura, the receptionist at the Guide Dog Centre at that time, even typed some of the letters for me. Everyone was helpful.

One day we visited the vet in town for the dogs to have a routine health check. Each dog has a health record book, as it must be inoculated once a year and given a full medical examination every six months. I was given a recommended weight to maintain for Yasmin and told this was most important. I must not allow family members, friends or anyone to feed her tit-bits. An overweight Guide Dog does not work well, and it can cause health problems.

Towards the end of our four week training each student was examined by the Controller of the Centre. I set off on the test walk. The Controller and an instructor, other than my own, watched to see how I handled the dog, crossed roads, coped with off-kerb obstacles and free ran the dog. I knew I could be asked to do anything, which had been part of the training. Only when students fulfil all the requirements safely and satisfactorily are they allowed to become Guide Dog owners. Yasmin and I qualified two days before we were due to go home. We were asked to go to the Controller's office. He read the contract stating all the rules and conditions for Guide Dog ownership. I had to sign it.

Yasmin and I arrived home a week before Christmas. I had been invited to the Christmas party of the Visual Science Department at the Institute of Ophthalmology* in London. I thought it would be great fun to go on my own with Yasmin, our first big trip out. We had been taken on trains together during training at Wokingham. She had been taught to find the train door and the barrier at the station. We had learnt all the necessary safety aspects of railway stations and train journeys using Guide Dogs. I felt confident.

We set off for Redhill railway station. That was fine. I could still see the station, but not the step up to the entrance. Yasmin stopped at the step. I could still see the ticket office. When we reached it I said firmly to Yasmin, "This is the ticket office, the ticket office, the ticket office." From then on she would obey the command, "Find the ticket office."

Redhill station was poorly lit with three flights of grey concrete steps. At the top of the second flight I knew I had to turn left.

"Left," I commanded Yasmin. A few paces and again, "Left," before we went down to the platform for Victoria, London.

If I concentrated very hard I could read the indicator board, but could see nothing below or to the sides of it. Without Yasmin I could have wandered and fallen on to the railway track, or stumbled over the mail bags piled on the platform ready to be put on the train to Gatwick airport.

All went well. What a marvellous experience to arrive at Victoria station and find the crowds melting away. There was no struggling with my symbol cane. I was not knocked, banged or bumped. Everybody stood back for a Guide Dog. It was bliss. However I decided not to test my luck too much. I would take a taxi to the Institute. I knew the taxi stand was straight ahead and could instruct Yasmin.

"Straight."

"Left."

"This is the taxi rank, the taxi rank, the taxi rank."

It did not take many visits to London for Yasmin to learn this routine and lead me through it perfectly.

31

While I was standing in the taxi queue that first time a man touched me on the shoulder. "Your dog is absolutely beautiful," he said. "Here, take this. It's a pound of fillet steak. I was going to have it for my supper. You have it for your dog. She's amazing." I was left standing holding a plastic bag containing a pound of fillet steak. Arriving at the Institute I asked John Marshall if I could use his fridge.

"Why?"

"I have some fillet steak here."

"Well, you'll have to make space for it among the eyes."

When it was time to go home I completely forgot to take the steak with me.

I moved house the following February 1978. My instructor from Wokingham arrived soon afterwards. We decided together on the new routes for me to walk with Yasmin. Routes which would be useful and safe. This meant going into town many times to learn not only the way but also the different shops.

"Yasmin, this is the butcher's, the butcher's."

Yasmin was a bright young dog and learnt very quickly. If we did overshoot a doorway there was always a friendly arm to guide us back.

Yasmin became my constant companion. She was always willing to work, no matter what time of the day or night. She came with me when I visited the Branches of the Society. She went on trains, buses, taxis and even on aeroplanes. She went everywhere I needed to go and was invaluable to me. Sometimes we travelled all night taking the sleeper train to Scotland. When we flew to Ireland we were upgraded to first class immediately and always given the front row to ourselves so that Yasmin had space to stretch out with a plentiful supply of water.

On one trip to Ireland the Captain welcomed the passengers aboard, adding, "I would also like to welcome a good-looking blonde Guide Dog called Yasmin." We landed at Dublin airport to find that Aer Lingus had sent one of their own cars to take us across the tarmac to customs where my suitcases were waiting for me.

That was one of many trips to Ireland where I stayed with friends on their farm. Yasmin loved these visits. She was completely free having a holiday from working as a Guide Dog. She was fascinated by the cattle and would sit looking at them.

However capable Yasmin was I never forgot the fact she was a dog. Her natural instinct was to scavenge. One day we were walking at a steady speed along Oxford Street in London. A passer-by tapped me on the shoulder,

"Excuse me, do you realise your Guide Dog is following two pigeons carrying a slice of bread between them?"

We had a frightening experience on one journey as Yasmin and I travelled by ourselves on the night-sleeper train from Scotland. Suddenly there was a great commotion; the sound of people running up and down the corridor shouting, slamming doors, and opening windows. A steward came along to my carriage.

"You just stay in here. There are football hooligans fighting on the train. Somebody has been stabbed. Police are boarding the train."

We were held up at Carlisle for about three or four hours. I was worried about Yasmin needing to 'Spend'. Anticipating my predicament the steward arrived, offering to get off the train with Yasmin and me. We found a rough grass patch for Yasmin, and returning to the carriage I was asked to stay there.

On another train journey I was accompanied by my Aunt Jessie.

Yasmin befriended the man sitting opposite to us in the railway carriage. He informed us he was a member of the team responsible for the television programme 'The Wombles of Wimbledon'.

"Who or what are they?" whispered my aunt. "I never met them when I lived there."

I still had a little sight in those days. In fact I could still read print. Other passengers could not understand why I had a Guide Dog lying at my feet and a newspaper on my lap.

One Monday afternoon in September 1987, I heard the vet sigh. She continued examining Yasmin. Then very quietly she said, "Lynda, I'm sorry, but I think Yasmin has a growth in her left eye. I would like it checked out by the senior veterinary surgeon at the Animal Health Trust in Newmarket." Feeling nothing but dread we drove Yasmin to Newmarket the next day. I knew Dr Keith Barnet, Consultant of Ophthalmology in animals and the senior veterinary surgeon for GDBA. He was a member of the Society's Medical Advisory Board and in 1982 we had awarded him a grant of £10,000 to provide kennels as part of a large project of the Medical Research Council to study progressive retinal atrophy in dogs as a model for RP in people. After examining Yasmin he confirmed the diagnosis. There was only one thing he could do. He would have to remove the cancerous growth and the eye. That would mean the end of her working days as a Guide Dog. I was deeply saddened as I remembered what a wonderful companion she had been. Yasmin had worked for ten years, and won the hearts of all who knew her. Whenever we travelled together Yasmin was always the centre of attention.

However, she lived quite happily for a further three years with only one eye, enjoying her retirement with me.

I had been so attached to Yasmin I wasn't sure I wanted to replace her, but by Christmas I realised my independence in going out on my own had gone. I needed another Guide Dog.

'Blue Peter', the BBC children's television programme, was sponsoring a Guide Dog, a brood bitch called Goldie. Eventually she had eight puppies. They appeared on the programme regularly from the day after they were born until they went to their puppy walkers six weeks later. Children named the dogs: Amber, Honey, Fergie, Bruno, Holly, Snowy, Bonnie and Bonzo. Throughout the next eighteen months the dogs were shown on the Blue Peter programme at various stages of their training.

One afternoon I was sitting with Yasmin at my feet listening to the television. One of Goldie's puppies, Fergie, now a young dog, appeared on the programme, training with her new owner. Together with many other viewers I had admired the training of Goldie's puppies. There was the occasion when Derek Freeman, the breeding manager of GDBA, had fired a toy gun when they were eight weeks old to see if the noise startled them. It did for one ball of fur which trudged off unhappily, but this was soon remedied by the puppy walker. It was Snowy. I did not know then but he was to become my next Guide Dog.

Valentine's Day, February 1988, the day I was told, whilst training at the GDBA Centre, that I was to have a magnificent dog, a long-haired retriever, nearly white, called Snowy. One of Goldie's puppies of Blue Peter fame. He was a little bigger than Yasmin, but very quiet and a first class worker. Training the second time around was much easier because I knew what to expect. As I had moved to Northamptonshire by this time I went to the Centre at Edmond's Court, Leamington. It was a converted old manor house with lots of steps and long corridors. While I was there the local television team came to film Snowy. He had been trained as a country dog, which I needed having moved to the country. He was introduced to sheep, cows and horses as we crossed fields. Nothing perturbed him. He took no notice of other animals, not even a cat.

As before, Magnus, my instructor at the Centre, visited me at home until Snowy and I were familiar with the routes and the local shops in nearby Towcester. The village where I lived had a post office and a butcher's shop. Snowy soon found his way around the village and enjoyed the long country walks we took.

Snowy was used to the camera and for Christmas 1988 his photograph appeared on the front cover of the Guide Dogs for the Blind Dogalogue as their Christmas catalogue is called. He was also featured on a Christmas card.

On their third birthday the eight puppies were reunited with Goldie in the Blue Peter studio. Derek Freeman arrived to see that all his dogs behaved. I was told I must be there by 2.00pm ready for the programme to go on air at 5.00pm. At four o'clock Derek decided all the dogs ought to go and 'Spend'. We went to the Blue Peter garden. Off came the harnesses, the collars and leads. The dogs thought this was great. They pounded away, mud flying and they rolled. Aghast we retreated to the dressing-rooms. One room for two dogs and their owners. We had to clean them up and be back in the studio before 4.45pm. The programme went out live. To the relief of everyone all the dogs behaved well. Their birthday cake was an upside down bowl, which had been iced, with candles on it. Underneath were dog biscuits! The following Christmas a photograph of these celebrations appeared in the Blue Peter Annual.

On two occasions Snowy and I met the patron of GDBA, HRH the Princess Alexandra. She opened the new rehabilitation unit at their Centre in Leamington. After the ceremony I was invited, together with several other Guide Dog owners, to have tea with her. Then one spring I met her again when I was invited to attend a reception at St. James's Palace to mark the official launch of Action for Blind People.

Like Yasmin, Snowy was my constant companion. He appeared on several television programmes with me. By the time he was ten years old the GDBA had introduced the rule that all Guide Dogs must retire at ten years of age. I was not happy about this. He was in good health and working perfectly, but he had to be retired. He had five happy years of retirement with me, walking the country routes without a harness and spending time in the Society's office under one of the desks. He was an excellent Guide Dog, and along with Yasmin will be remembered by all my friends and family.

It was through Snowy I met Susan and Paul Freeland when they attended a committee meeting of the Towcester Branch for the GDBA. Susan and Paul are American and were working in England for a period of three years. They missed their golden retriever, left behind in the United States, so much that after meeting Snowy they decided to become puppy walkers for the GDBA. They puppy walked three dogs before returning to America.

Unfortunately the last one, Fern, a black Labrador, was rejected as a Guide Dog. The GDBA contacted Susan in America to ask her if they would like Fern as a pet. I made the travel arrangements and Fern arrived as a surprise birthday present for Paul.

———◆———

Snowy's replacement was another retriever named Kimber. As it was my third dog and the GDBA had begun domiciliary training I did not have to go away. Unfortunately this dog was not suitable to be a Guide Dog. I persevered for three years, but as her work continued to be inconsistent and unreliable she had to be retired. The GDBA found her a good home.

This experience undermined my confidence, but it was soon restored when I trained with my fourth Guide Dog. He is a handsome black Labrador; a big dog called Laddie, weighing 100lbs or just over 45 kilograms. He is a gentle giant and very good. He was a marvellous millennium birthday gift for me. When he was introduced to Snowy, who was almost fifteen years old, Laddie treated him with the respect a retired Guide Dog deserved. Nick Toni, Laddie's trainer, travelled from Leamington, the Guide Dog Centre, every week day, to teach Laddie the routes around Pond Farmhouse. It took Laddie only a few weeks to learn his way about. Early in February 2001 Snowy was diagnosed with an incurable disease and had to be put to sleep. A week later Laddie and I went into the Paddock to scatter Snowy's ashes.

The following June I moved to Stony Stratford. By this time I had lost the last vestige of sight. I was completely blind, so Laddie and I were faced with a huge challenge. Both of us had to learn new routes now. The GDBA had changed the boundaries to their areas, which meant Laddie and I came under the Wokingham Centre. Late that summer I started training with Alison Rampling. She is a qualified rehabilitation officer for the blind and was an apprentice Guide Dog mobility instructor then. We purchased street maps of Stony Stratford and after she had worked out the safest and most suitable routes for us she marked them on the maps with a special marker. She reproduced the maps, using thermal imaging, so that the roads I would use became raised. I could then trace them with my fingers and so memorise the routes. Laddie soon learnt the different routes to the High Street. He can identify the shops I need and will lead me safely to them.

Laddie and I have made many new friends during his free runs in the park. Some are two-legged and some four. We are thinking of starting the Stony Stratford black Labrador club. Laddie's special playmate is a black Labrador called Sam. They have great fun together free running in the park. However if we meet while Laddie is working in harness he is not distracted when he sees Sam. According to Sam's owner, Diane, Laddie simply gives a small wag of his tail. Through the dogs Diane and I have become great friends.

In 2005 Laddie was made the GDBA regional 'Guide Dog of the Year', for his exceptional work and outstanding loyalty and devotion to his owner. On two occasions, within a year, I have been knocked down by cars as they were reversed out of driveways. Each time he remained by my side.

I am delighted to say I have a remarkable working Guide Dog who can be trusted totally as he helps me to find the way.

Chapter 5

GRASS ROOTS
The Importance of Branches

"No man is an Island, entire of itself;
every man is a piece of the Continent, a part of the main."
John Donne 1572-1631

There was a buzz of excitement in the air. Everyone felt it. It was electric. Our first Annual General Meeting had just finished. It was a warm summer afternoon in June 1977 and people were standing in little groups; some gathered around a speaker from earlier in the day. All were talking animatedly. They had been fired by the talks they had heard. What could they do?

Many went home determined to get together with other RP sufferers in their area and form a local group. They were sure it would help them to feel less isolated. More important still, they wanted to do something practical to support the research and all the efforts to find a treatment and eventual cure for RP.

A few groups already existed. After listening to my interview on Radio 4's 'In Touch' programme the previous year Joe Richardson and Frank Boreman came to see me. They told me there were a number of RP sufferers in Kent who, together with themselves, had linked up to form a group. They were interested in becoming affiliated to the Society. John and Judith Marshall travelled with me to Kent to talk to this group. I will never forget seeing for the first time so many people all in different stages of RP. Some, like me, were in the early stages of the disease, and were moving around the room quite easily on their own. Others had the detestable white cane while a few were guided holding the arm of a friend. "Was this to be my future?" I wondered ruefully.

On another occasion the three of us went to Gravesend for a dance organised by the same group to be held at the Working Men's Club. This time we were confronted by Cowboys and Red Indians! A pint of beer was put in my hand. As the jazz band swung into action getting louder and louder, so the room became hotter and hotter. However, as I said goodbye at the end of the evening I was assured a lot of money had been raised for our research fund.

I visited that group in Kent countless times. Once, when I stayed with Joe and Helena Richardson I slept in their daughter's bedroom while she was away at boarding school. The room was charmingly decorated with curtains, duvet cover and lampshades all matching. Their daughter was totally blind and deaf, but I was sure she would sense the atmosphere of the room and be aware of the love and effort her parents had poured into it for her.

"Why should blind people be deprived of a beautiful environment just because they can't see it?" I mused to myself.

Amongst the first batch of letters, after the 'In Touch' programme in 1976, was one from Denis and Teresa Carter telling me about their two children, both of whom had RP and a hearing loss. They wanted to meet other families facing similar difficulties and share experiences of bringing up children with RP. Catherine was now sixteen and Andrew thirteen. Their enthusiasm to start a local Avon group was apparent when I spoke to them on the telephone.

It was not long before they invited me to stay with them so that I could meet the group. It was a delight to hear about the successful Bring and Buy Sale and all the local support this group had generated from shopkeepers and various clubs in the area.

After a delicious dinner cooked by Teresa we settled down for a relaxing evening.

"Have you always lived in the Devizes area?" I asked Denis.

"No, I was born in London. We then moved to Hove where Teresa and I, both aged eight years, met in Primary school. Although I became an accountant working in London, I hankered after a career in farming and ended up with my own farm consulting business here."

He also told me that his other great interest was in politics and in 1967 he had stood, unsuccessfully, for Parliament.

How could I know then that in 1987 he was to become a life peer for the Labour Party and that ten years later Prime Minister Tony Blair would ask him to be the Government's Chief Whip in the House of Lords. We would meet Denis at Westminster on more than one occasion in the future.

Our thoughts turned to London that year of 1976. Surely anyone in London with an interest in RP would want to join a group. We were right. I sat thrilled as more and more people entered the room for their first meeting. I remember some of them clearly. A tall, attractive young lady attended. She had been a model until the day she fell off the end of the catwalk. There was something wrong with her eyesight. She, too, was diagnosed with Retinitis Pigmentosa. She wanted to help us and as both of us could still see a little she became a great companion.

Another lady came up to me and said, "My dear, you won't do any good, you don't wear a hat. Anybody who is a lady running committees wears a hat." I didn't wear a hat then and I've never worn a hat since to any of our meetings, committee or otherwise. Years later the Society would have reason to be grateful to this lady.

James Hudson, who was one of our original Trustees, invited this London group to Sunday lunch at his London home so that they could meet members of the medical panel and ask them questions. For most, it was the first time they had ever had an opportunity like this to mingle with the professionals and chat to them leisurely at a social gathering. John Marshall together with Professors Alan Bird and Geoffrey Arden were there. It was from this party, hearing the same questions asked again and again, that an idea developed. We would publish a booklet 'Your Questions Answered'. Then everyone in the Society could benefit.

I woke early, as usual, on the morning of my birthday in November 1977. It was to be a day packed with engagements. I tried to analyse my emotions: anticipation, apprehension, a measure of excitement.

Mary Guest and I travelled together to Birmingham. We talked of all that had happened since our first meeting two years earlier. Although there had been many encouragements we both knew it was only the beginning of all our hopes and plans. There was a long way to go.

Roger and Margaret Green met us. Roger has RP. He and Margaret had attended our first AGM and had started a Midlands Branch. We were expected at the Midlands Eye Hospital in Birmingham that afternoon.

Professor James Crews welcomed us at the hospital and showed us some of the equipment they were using. He was interested in RP and had been a great help to Roger and Margaret. In the years ahead he supported the Society constantly in various ways until his death in 1994. After serving for a number of years on our Management Committee he became a Trustee.

We went on to Aston University where I met Neville Dressdale. He was working to develop ways Closed Circuit Television (CCTV) could help visually impaired people with reading material. CCTV was to play a prominent part in the lives of our members. It can magnify or reduce the size of print. What is more it can print black on white or reverse it to white on black, which some people with RP find more helpful.

In the evening Jessie Mole and John Marshall joined us for the meeting of the Midlands Branch. There were over seventy people there. As I looked out over the sea of faces my mouth became dry. Would I have to address them? I was introduced to Professor Crews' wife Annie. She too, promised to support the Society. Their two young daughters presented me with a little gift for my birthday. Everyone was friendly and encouraging. I soon felt at ease.

Ken Whetton, the fundraiser for the Branch, staggered us all by handing me a cheque for £1,000. This was a vast sum in 1977. It was the largest amount we had received so far. Ken's wife, Agnes, had RP. He had worked very hard organising numerous events to raise this money. He was never short of ideas and always had plenty of willing helpers. His energy and appearance reminded me of Arthur Askey. There was more to follow. James Crews' daughter Bridget gave me £200 which she had raised at her school.

Meanwhile in the West Country Mary Tombs and her family had been equally busy organising a Branch in Exeter. Mary had also been at our first AGM. I was driven by John and Judith Marshall to meet this group. Yasmin, my first Guide Dog, accompanied us and lay under the top table with her head poking out from underneath the long tablecloth. While John was speaking she slept peacefully. When I began to speak, unknown to me, she started to yawn much to the amusement of the people sitting in the front three rows. I was perplexed. What had I said to cause such merriment? At last somebody explained.

Again the meeting of this Branch was well attended with some people travelling from as far away as Truro. Attempts to start a Branch in Cornwall failed, but there were always loyal members who were prepared to travel to the different venues in Devon.

London, the South-East, the Midlands, the South-West; where next I wondered.

"How do you feel about coming up to Glasgow?" a softly spoken Glaswegian voice asked at the other end of the telephone one day in 1978. It was Irene Solomons who often telephoned me. Irene had not taken long to ring around all our members in Scotland in order to start a Branch. In no time at all she had discovered that Professor Wallace Foulds was involved in RP research at the Western Eye Infirmary in Glasgow, and she arranged to meet him there.

As I boarded the 11.00pm night sleeper train at Euston station, holding Yasmin's harness in one hand and my red suitcase in the other, I looked forward to seeing Irene again. In spite of her RP she spent much of her time working tirelessly to nurture the Branch. It grew and grew largely due to her inspiration. When Irene bade me farewell at the end of my first visit she said, "Promise you will return to Scotland as soon as we have more

Branches."

I did return, again on the night sleeper. Arriving at Edinburgh railway station, on a bitterly cold day with snow falling, Dr Cliff Beevers, the chairman of the newly formed Branch, and Dr Shomi Bhattacharya, our research worker, ran along the platform to meet me. Shomi, wearing a shirt and sleeveless sweater, seemed oblivious of the cold. He was so enthusiastic about his research work he talked non-stop in the taxi all the way to the University. I didn't have lunch that day until I had been all around Shomi's laboratory. How could I possibly know at the time that Shomi would play such a vital role in RP research?

On another occasion during a whistle-stop tour of four Scottish Branches I visited Aberdeen, the Granite City. I felt I was returning to my roots on my father's side. I asked my host and hostess Ann and Les Anderson, who founded the Grampian Branch, if they would take me to Rose Cottage where my great aunt Mary had lived. We arrived early for the Branch meeting at the premises of the Grampian Blind Society. I wanted to find out if my blind great aunt had been registered with them. We soon found her name, Mary Henderson. The three days spent in Aberdeen included interviews for BBC Radio Aberdeen, Northsound and Grampian Television.

On a subsequent visit to Glasgow a research worker at Strathclyde University pounced on me.

"We'll have some of your blood for our work, Lynda. Remember, no breakfast for you tomorrow."

I was not allowed to eat anything the next morning before going back to the University to give blood for the research work into RP being carried out there.

It was April 1985 and we were travelling to Aberdeen for the first

BRPS Scottish Conference. Many of our Scottish members felt it was too far to travel to London for our AGM but they wanted the same opportunity to hear about medical research into RP and meet people from other Branches to exchange news and ideas. A pattern emerged that Scottish Conferences would be held on alternate years. Gerry Malone, the Member of Parliament for Aberdeen at the time, was present at this first conference. John Marshall confronted him.

"Why had the DHSS withdrawn their grant towards our administration costs?" Although we had received this grant for six years it was never renewed.

One Friday evening, four years later, together with about one hundred people, we attended a glittering function in the splendour of Glasgow City Chambers. We were marking the opening of the Scottish Conference hosted by the Strathclyde Branch.

We adapted to the change of atmosphere the following morning as the world of research was explained to us by the speakers dedicated to their work on our behalf. Professor Wallace Foulds, Shomi Bhattacharya and Dr Carolyn Converse from the Scottish Universities were joined on the platform by John Marshall and Tony Moore from the South for the Question and Answer session. Trevan Hingston, BRPS Chairman, conducted the business meeting. Bob Gould, the Society's Welfare Officer, led a discussion on Welfare matters.

Aberdeen, Glasgow, Edinburgh were all venues for a BRPS Scottish Conference. We wanted to support them as part of the BRPS family.

Ever since childhood I had been drawn to Scotland personally and these visits to our Scottish Branches and Conferences gave me particular pleasure.

———◆———

As Branches sprang up around the country I realised that it was important that a range of speakers visited them in order to keep their enthusiasm alive. It would give them the opportunity of meeting experts in all aspects of RP. The most popular request, always, was for speakers involved with medical research.

The network grew. There were thirty Branches spreading from London and the South-East to Scotland, across to Northern Ireland, back to the North-West of England, Wales and down to the South-West. I visited most of them, sometimes leaving home at 6.00am. I met the Mayors of many towns and cities and was interviewed by numerous local television and radio teams.

Time and again at Branch meetings I met social workers and others, both professionals and volunteers, who worked with the visually handicapped. This helped to build good relationships, particularly between local hospitals, social services with their mobility officers and Branch members. A wealth of information was gained by having these people at meetings, and they, in turn, learnt about the BRPS and the support it offers to people with RP.

Everywhere I went I was made welcome. I met so many people. They were from various walks of life, some had RP and others were their family members or friends. I stayed in their homes; the main topic of conversation always was RP. I was convinced that the Branches were crucial to the work of the Society. They are, in fact, the grass roots of it.

The telephone rang one evening. It was Aunt Jessie. She had an idea. She would like to establish a meeting for Branch chairmen twice a year. She set about inviting them to the first meeting which was held in Birmingham. The twice yearly meetings became a pattern with London as the most accessible place for everyone.

Many subjects were covered, but it was at these meetings the members urged us to update the rules of the Society for the Branches. Nothing had been written in great detail and we felt this should be done.

My aunt also wanted to give them an opportunity to meet socially in a congenial, relaxed atmosphere. Her annual Garden Party for Branch chairmen and women in her garden at Sunningwell became a tradition.

At the time of writing, as I look back, I realise that in the past, talks at Branch meetings enabled members to learn about all aspects of RP. The arrival of the Internet now means information is quickly and easily accessible. This may be one reason why some Branches have closed in recent years. The Management Committee, together with the Trustees, decided that one of their members should take responsibility for Branch affairs in an attempt to give them more support. This post has been held by members who have had experience in running a Branch.

Although the Branches are fewer in number today, they continue the momentum of fundraising. This is as strong as ever.

Chapter 6

MONEY, MONEY, MONEY
Fundraising and Grants

"If I were a rich man ..."
Fiddler on the Roof. Joseph Stein b.1912

"Have we picked enough yet?" came the plaintive cry of a tired child. Seven little eager helpers who had set off to pick strawberries for my first fundraising event were becoming bored. Friends, neighbours, family members had responded enthusiastically to my suggestion, "Let's give a garden party, to raise some funds. There's a lot of stationery to buy." As complete amateurs we were delighted with our profit of £187, a lot of money in 1975. It enabled us to open our first bank account.

Administrative expenses were growing rapidly. There was only one way to generate a regular income and that was to introduce a membership subscription of £1. By November of the same year the Society's balance stood at £230. Four months later that figure had risen to £897. Today the balance is well over a million pounds at any one time.

―◆―

As soon as Stanley Saunders, an accountant, joined the Society he was invited to become treasurer, releasing Jessie of this responsibility. Three years later in 1980 Norman Pampel, also a qualified accountant, took over from Stanley Saunders. He was treasurer for fourteen years and the skill with which he moved funds around the money market amazed us all. Norman and Nina's son Mark has Usher Syndrome. After Norman retired in 1994 we were fortunate to find George Thompson. He and Jo also have a son with RP.

Much of our income has been generated by our members, but not all. I remember trudging ankle deep in mud after a night of rain as we walked around the 'See by Touch' exhibition at the Agricultural Centre, Stoneleigh near Coventry in 1979. Dr John Gill, who worked at the Warwickshire research unit for the blind at Coventry University, was the prime organiser of the exhibition.

The main aim of the day was to give blind and partially sighted people the opportunity of touching objects and animals outside their experience of normal life. I heard blind school children exclaim as they were told, "This is a sheep." Stroking the sheep gently they obtained an idea of its size, and the woolly texture of its coat. Likewise, they were introduced to other farm animals of various sizes and shapes. They also enjoyed climbing on the tractors and even up onto a combine harvester.

During lunch I was introduced to a representative from the Department of Health and Social Security who offered to accompany me on the train back to London. On the journey home, as I enthused about the Society and its aims, he suggested I apply for a DHSS grant to help with the cost of administration. I had no idea such grants existed. I bombarded him with questions.

"Where do I apply and to whom?"

He handed me a business card saying, "To me at my department."

The next morning I wrote to him enclosing a copy of our

Newsletter and our only publicity leaflet. To my joy a grant of £3,000 per annum, increasing later to £5,000 per annum, was offered to enable the Society to expand over the next six years. At least now we could feel that our administration costs would be covered.

Money for medical research was kept quite separate in a different account and was raised by our members in numerous and ingenious ways. Countless sponsored events were organised. Walks, cycle rides, swimathons, piano playing, and a tour of Anglican cathedrals to name but a few. Mountains were conquered, parachute jumps were achieved, not to mention bungee jumps and abseiling.

The first London marathon will always remain a vivid memory. Cheered by more than one million spectators a member of the Society, Dennis Moore, finished the London Gillette Marathon, held on Sunday 29th March 1981, in a time of 3 hours 55 minutes.

To make sure I could be at the start at Greenwich to wish Dennis luck, Joe and Helena Richardson of the Kent Branch drove up early from Gravesend. It was an incredible sight at Greenwich Park to see the field of 7,000 contestants awaiting the gruelling task of running the 26 miles from Greenwich to Constitution Hill. The smell of liniment filled the air.

We thought we would never find Dennis among the crowds. An understanding policeman led us into the enclosure on learning we wanted to find the only blind runner. I am sure he thought we were looking so anxious because we had the competitor's Guide Dog! We soon found Dennis and his two-legged guide Wally Scott as they sported RP T-shirts, and at 9am they were sent on their way by the boom of a 25 pound cannon being fired.

It was thrilling to watch Dennis and Wally, three hours later, rounding the corner into Constitution Hill. Ever since then members of the Society have taken part in the London marathon to raise money for our research fund.

Further money for medical research was generated by individual initiatives. One such initiative changed the course of my life. After a visit to the Coventry Branch in 1983 with Janet Silver we called to see her brother Leslie, who was a partner in the Company, Cantor & Silver, (later to become Cantor & Nissel Ltd) which manufactured contact lenses.

The following morning Leslie's partner David Cantor telephoned me. He explained he had a collection of vintage vehicles, including a van of which there were a hundred replica models. He planned to sell these models to raise money for our medical research fund. Two months later over lunch he presented me with a cheque for £1,000. Within a few years David and I were married.

Another initiative was taken by Jenny Rudge who was a familiar figure in Reigate library as she sat studying the Directory of Grant-making Trusts. In 1985 there were no short cuts to obtaining names and addresses of Trusts concerned with medical research into the prevention of blindness. She spent hours on this exercise.

Jenny and Alan Rudge have a daughter, Penny, who was diagnosed with Usher Syndrome at the age of thirteen. Jenny decided to raise funds for medical research in her own particular way. She liked the thought of writing to Grant-making Trusts appealing for money and we soon saw the results of her first batch of letters.

"It's about time we bought Jenny a copy of the Directory of Grant-making Trusts, so that she can work at home. It is a vital tool of fundraising." The Trustees unanimously agreed.

Today the age of computers has simplified the work of sending out appeal letters. Jenny is still writing them, and after twenty years has raised a total of £432,553.

Similarly Frank Rogers of our Plymouth sub-branch had been writing appeal letters to local organisations on behalf of BRPS. Most had been ignored, but some had brought in a small donation.

Frank then appealed on local radio (Plymouth Sound) for volunteers to help sell raffle tickets in a local supermarket in 1985. Consequently he heard of the South Devon and Cornwall Institute for the Blind and wrote to them.

In his letter he mentioned the many research projects that we were financing. The result was a telephone call inviting Frank to attend their next meeting and asking if he could bring along someone who could give them details of our research programme. I suggested that perhaps John Marshall might agree to attend and as a result John caught the train to Plymouth.

His talk and answers to their queries gave them all the information they needed. The committee retired to another room and after half an hour's private deliberation invited Frank and John to join them. They would finance a PhD research studentship at £10,000 per year for three years – a total of £30,000. Frank pinched himself to make sure he wasn't dreaming.

The South Devon and Cornwall Institute for the Blind was founded in 1861 to provide services for blind people in the area. They operate a flourishing workshop for the blind where sails for yachts are made. Several of their employees in that workshop had RP, which was the reason for their interest in BRPS. The Institute continues to support RP research to this day.

An enterprising family left me in no doubt about their commitment to fundraising for our medical research. I first met Colin and Linda McArthur at the inaugural meeting of the Essex Branch in 1980. Colin took early retirement at the age of thirty-six, due to RP, in 1986. As well as running a nursery school Linda was a busy mother with four young sons, two of whom are twins. A fifth son was born later.

Linda and Colin published the following 'ABC of Fundraising Ideas' in our Newsletter.

ABC of Fundraising Ideas

A. Abseiling, Assault course, Austerity lunch, Auction, Awful tie competition.
B. Barbecue, Ball, Barn dance, Banquet, Bring & Buy, Bed push, Balloon race, Bingo, Burns' Night party, Beard shave.
C. Country show, Challenges and contests, Car boot sales, Cheese & wine party, Coffee morning, Collections, Cake sale.
D. Dinner, Disco, Dance, Dance-a-thon, Darts match, Dog show.
E. Easter egg hunt.
F. Fancy dress party, Flower arranging, Fashion show, Fete, Fifties night, Fish 'n' chip evening, Flower festival, Fun run.
G. Guessing games (name the doll, weight of the cake), Garage sale, Garden party.
H. Hook-a-duck, Hoop-la, Hallowe'en party.
I. It's a knockout, In memoriam donation (in lieu of flowers).
J. Jam making, Jumble sale, Jazz event, Jellied eel eating.
K. Karaoke, Kidnap and ransom, Knees-up party.
L. Lecture (local personality), Lunch, Look-a-like competition.
M. Millennium party, Make-up demo, Mid-summer ball, Mile of pennies.
N. Nearly new sale.
O. Opera evening, One day fast.
P. Pub cards, Pennies in a jar, Palm reading, Pancake race,

	Plant sale, Pram race, Pub crawl, Parachute jump, Picnic.
Q.	Quiz night, Quasar challenge.
R.	Raffle, Race night.
S.	Sponsored Stalls & Sideshows, Store collection, Sherry morning, Skittles, Sunday brunch, Supper party, Swim-a-thon.
T.	Tombolas, Table sales, Tandem/cycle ride, Talent contest, Tea dance, Teddy bears' picnic, Tug of War, Ten pin bowling.
U.	Ugly face pulling.
V.	Vicars and clowns party, Valentine's day dance.
W.	Walks (sponsored), Wheel of fortune, Whist drive, Wine tasting.
X.	X marks the spot, Xmas cards (Webb Ivory).
Y.	Yard of Ale competition, Yo-Yo competition.
Z.	Zoo trips (or any day out), Zoo quiz.

It was not long before Colin and Linda joined the Management Committee. In 1993 they proposed an ambitious scheme.

"Linda and I would like to start a national raffle," Colin announced.

"Are you sure? It would involve a lot of work. You would have to ask companies to donate prizes, obtain a licence, print the tickets, mail them to members, keep accounts."

"We're sure we can do it. The boys will help." And they did. That first year the McArthur family raised £6,200 from the raffle for our research fund.

They have continued to this day to co-ordinate an annual national raffle for us; raising well over £100,000 after all expenses have been paid. Their cheerful willingness to help, whatever the occasion, is a great encouragement.

A new opening for fundraising came with David's clever idea of obtaining funding from optical companies.

Kelvin Lenses Ltd made a generous promise in 1985. For every voucher returned by a customer purchasing a starter pack of contact lens solution the firm would give ten pence to BRPS. Thirty thousand vouchers were sent out.

Each year David and I travelled vast distances visiting numerous Optical Trade Exhibitions. We could not believe how the miles had clocked up. David always had a stand promoting his Company, Cantor & Silver, at these exhibitions, and usually managed to arrange a space for me to publicise BRPS.

I looked forward to the social events in the evenings. At the Conference Dinner we decided to raffle the Sinclair car which had been donated to the Society. As this was a spontaneous gesture and we had no raffle tickets, we asked people to place in a bucket a five pound note marked with their initials. Yasmin and I were asked to make the draw. Yasmin wasted no time sniffing out the five pound note which had been soaked in gravy! The bucket contained £1,500.

On another evening we happened to sit opposite a representative from the pharmaceutical company Allergan. "Do you think Allergan would sponsor new collecting boxes for BRPS?" David asked him.

"Possibly, as long as their name appears on each box," he replied.

Some time later David greeted me with the words, "Wonderful news Lynda. Allergan has agreed to donate £3,000 to cover the cost of new collecting boxes. Their representatives will deliver them to opticians and hospital ophthalmic departments when they visit them to sell their products."

As soon as the new collecting boxes arrived at the office in 1986 it was like sitting in a field of ripe rape seed. Every space was covered with bright yellow boxes. What fun we had packing them ready for mailing to Branches and individual members.

Optical manufacturers, who supply contact lenses, solutions for cleaning them, frames for spectacles and any related equipment, supported us by advertising in our new annual Handbook.

The revenue from these advertisements not only met the cost of this Handbook, which was first produced in 1988, but also gave us a profit for our medical research fund. Our accounts, a report by the Trustees, grants made by the Society for medical research, an update of that research and a list of the names and addresses of Branch officers were included in the Handbook. Photographs reproduced for the cover introduced a personal link with members. After ten years it became increasingly difficult to sell advertising space and we replaced it with an A4 folder with six inserts. This proved to be cost effective, as only those sections which required updating were reprinted.

Many of our members have been motivated to raise funds for our medical research because they have a family member or friend with RP. Invitations to some memorable lunch parties came from two such members. Sir Henry Jones, whose wife had RP, was Master of the Clothworkers' Company and Chairman of their Foundation in 1985. The Clothworkers' Foundation was set up in 1977 as a registered charity by the Clothworkers' Company, which replaced the ancient City of London Clothworkers' Livery Company. This was the twelfth of the 'Great Twelve', established by a Royal Charter issued in 1528 by King Henry VIII. The Governors of the Foundation distribute money allocated by the

Company for the support of charities. Sir Henry nominated BRPS to be considered for an award that year.

I was invited to receive a cheque at their annual lunch party to be held in their magnificent buildings in the City of London. Soon after we arrived for lunch Yasmin came nose to nose with a large police dog in the ladies' cloakroom. He was another working dog, but with a different job, sniffing out explosives. After the building was given the all-clear by security we proceeded up the grand marble staircase, into the dining room, to await the arrival of HRH the Princess Royal, who was representing 'Save the Children Fund'. Pre-luncheon drinks were served while we mingled with the other guests.

"You have a lovely dog," said a familiar voice as Yasmin was given a royal pat.

How I envied the Princess' ability to give such an interesting after lunch speech without reference to any notes. Both she and I were given substantial donations for our respective charities presented by Sir Henry. I came away with a cheque for £10,000. Some years later our Newsletter was sponsored by the Clothworkers' Foundation for a three year period. I therefore enjoyed being invited to their prestigious functions on three more occasions, one being in the presence of HRH the Princess Alexandra.

Another member was Carol Estrin, whose son has RP. She led a group of young married women living in Edgware, Middlesex and formed 'The Daylight Committee'. One of their first events was a successful barbecue-disco. Two hundred and thirty guests gave them a profit of £2,600. Their next brainwave was 'Keep Fit' lunches. 'Mad' Lizzie Webb of TV AM ran the keep fit sessions. So started the annual 'Daylight Ladies' Luncheons'. I well remember these elegant lunches; particularly the occasion when they included a fashion show. The superior raffle prizes donated so generously by them frequently raised more than £11,000.

Two national appeals were made on behalf of the Society on Radio 4.

Curled up in a chair on a cold Sunday morning in November 1986, I listened to a voice I had heard so often on the Radio 4 programme 'Thought for the Day'. Rabbi Lionel Blue was speaking on 'The Week's Good Cause' telling listeners about the progressive loss of sight from Retinitis Pigmentosa. This was an appeal to generate funds for our ambitious plan to develop a Helpline in addition to our medical research programme. The Helpline would enable sufferers to contact someone who understood their fears concerning the future. Years later I had the opportunity to thank Rabbi Lionel Blue personally, when he was appearing at Milton Keynes Theatre. The amount of mail that followed this Appeal was unbelievable. Donations ranged from coins wrapped in tissue paper to a cheque for £2,000. The grand total realised more than £24,000.

We were allowed to appeal for the Society on Radio 4's programme 'The Week's Good Cause' once again in 2001. This time our appeal was made by Rolf Harris. He told the story of Jessica, a young teenager who had battled with RP since she was four years old. Rolf described the difficulties Jessica faced in his usual compassionate way.

"Every charity seems to sell its own Christmas cards. Perhaps we should do the same. Think of the publicity. BRPS cards arriving in homes throughout the country."

The suggestion was greeted enthusiastically by the Management Committee. Choosing the designs was a nightmare and eventually the task was carried out by a Christmas card committee. Thus began an ongoing Society initiative to raise funds.

I will always remember our first Christmas card. I came home one day to find my hall filled with boxes from floor to ceiling. With some trepidation I opened the first box expecting to find packets of cards and envelopes. Not so. The flat sheets of cards needed folding and put together in packets of six with envelopes from another box.

"I must have some help," I thought. Two roads away I found a willing assistant in Jane Sellers, a young teenager who has Laurence-Moon-Bardet-Biedl Syndrome* as does her sister. We spent many summer evenings together folding and counting Christmas cards. After this first experience we arranged for a supplier to send them direct to our members.

In 1988 we had an unexpected opportunity when Rolf Harris offered to design our Christmas cards for the following year. He and his wife made us welcome when we visited their home one evening to collect the two designs.

He also lent us his oil painting of Queen Street, Maidenhead showing a horse-drawn carriage and cart. A limited edition of one hundred prints and packets of notelets were produced from this original painting. We were fortunate to have such a generous and unique gift.

Some Branch initiatives took me to different venues. Never having been to dog racing before, I was intrigued by an invitation to a sponsored dog race meeting at Romford stadium in aid of our research fund. Yasmin, my Guide Dog, was fascinated as she sat at the window of the restaurant looking down on the dogs racing around the track after the electric hare.

In Birmingham's 18th century cathedral a Mozart Bi-Centenary concert was given in aid of BRPS in December 1991. It was remarkable that this beautiful concert was conducted by someone with RP, Alan Davis.

From a cathedral to a Welsh castle at Craig-y-Nos. On this occasion in 1994 I was enthralled by the sounds of a Welsh Male Voice Choir who were singing for our research fund.

———◆◆———

According to our medical advisors what we really needed was our own laboratory for research into RP. They found just the right site in the Rayne Institute at St Thomas' Hospital, London. The initial target was a quarter of a million pounds to equip the laboratory and employ several research workers. This was the most enterprising project and biggest financial challenge we had faced so far. All the Trustees were asked to list their personal contacts with banks, large companies and all other possible donors. Appeal letters were sent out.

Dr Alan Rudge, one of our Trustees, contacted the charity department of his company, British Telecommunications. A representative of this department visited us at home. David and I explained, over lunch, why we needed such a laboratory. By the time she left she had promised a donation of £25,000 per annum for three years. This was a great encouragement, but we still had a long way to go.

An exciting venue for the formal launch of the appeal was arranged by Alan Rudge at the top of the British Telecoms Post Office Tower on 28th May 1992. Although it had been a restaurant open to the general public it was closed following a bomb attack by the IRA. Since then it has been used only on special occasions and security was tight. Everybody, including a number of celebrities and directors of industrial companies, wanted to come to see the spectacular views of London from a revolving restaurant so high in the air.

To make the event more memorable, an attempt was made on Jimmy Savile's 20 year old record for running up the 890 steps. Three people took up the challenge, Duke McKenzie, the British and former World Flyweight boxing champion, Michael Everard, President of the Chamber of Shipping and Kate Stephens, the Olympic yachtswoman, who has RP and won a gold medal at the Blind Sailing Regatta held in New Zealand. They all made it to the top, with Duke clipping 15 seconds off the old record of 6 minutes 36 seconds.

Our President, Sir Campbell Adamson, began his introduction by reading a telegram from Sir Jimmy Savile stating, "Don't break my record or I'll be round there with a couple of heavies."

Professor John Marshall explained the reasons for the new laboratory and the work that it would carry out. David Cantor told us how BRPS was the largest source of funds for RP research in the UK and announced that the amount pledged to the appeal to date was £117,000.

By the spring of the following year we had received £235,000. It was tantalising to be so close to our target with a shortfall of just £15,000. A few months later we were able to announce that our goal of £250,000 had been achieved.

The laboratory and a team were in place. As a next step we were eager to fund the new three year research project, led by our research scientist Dr Steve Jones. It aimed to develop a process for introducing corrective genetic material* into the appropriate cells within an eye. It was impossible to inject material into the nucleus of such a cell using a needle.

From time to time our fundraising receives a welcome boost. In 1996 the National Lottery Charities Board had a category, which allowed application for an award towards medical research under the heading 'Health, Disability and Care'. Filling in the forms for this application was the most daunting task Selwyn Higgins has undertaken for us. Night after night he burnt the midnight oil in order to complete them by the deadline. We rejoiced together when finally we heard that an award of £69,000 had been made to the Society.

Stephen Jones, who at the time of writing is the Society's Development Manager and has a son with RP, spent more than a year trying to obtain funding for a two year programme of research into gene therapy* led by Dr Robin Ali. As a result in May 2001 we heard that the pharmaceutical company Glaxo Smith Kline had awarded us £97,000 for this project.

A different way of raising funds for medical research came about through the Honourable Sophie Montgomery, one of our Trustees. She telephoned to tell me that, with the help of a close friend, she had managed to get the Society included in a group of six charities which would benefit from a Global Annual Charity Day. Little did I realise how memorable and profitable that Charity Day would prove to be.

The event was organised by a company called Garban Intercapital (ICAP), which provides a specialist interdealer broking service to commercial banks, investment banks and other 'liquidity providers' on the wholesale financial markets. With more than two thousand staff worldwide ICAP has a strong presence in London, New York, Tokyo and many other financial markets. On their annual Charity Day, ICAP gives away all of its revenues to six named charities.

To learn more about it Sophie and I were invited, with representatives of the other five charities, to a meeting in the Boardroom of ICAP in the City of London. We were asked to invite celebrities, who supported our work, to accompany us on the Charity Day. This would enhance the day ICAP was putting on for charities as far as the media was concerned. The young man sitting beside me immediately offered the services of Elton John.

When the day dawned, early in December 2002, it was bitterly cold. I donned my fur hat and set off for London with Kate Samwell and Yvonne Lennard from the BRPS office. We wondered what the day would bring forth.

Arriving at ICAP's premises we were taken on a tour of the trading floors. To our amusement we were greeted by the sight of money dealers in fancy dress to mark the spirit of the occasion. Orang-utans, a look-alike Elvis Presley, bunny girls, catwomen in skin-tight patent leather catsuits and other bizarre participants operated the rows and rows of computer screens. Photographers were everywhere.

The Society's celebrity joined us. Tom Watt, Lofty of 'EastEnders' fame, sports presenter and author. We were intrigued as we watched the traders in action. Buying and selling money on the financial markets of the world is intense, fast and utterly absorbing. They had no time to stop for lunch. Chinese waiters delivered take-away meals to their desks.

As we emerged from the lift on the way to our lunch in the Boardroom, I heard a voice nearby. Thinking Kate was beside me I asked, "Who's that?"

"They call me Elton John," came the reply.

"Lynda Cantor, nice to meet you."

After complimenting me on my hat he and his entourage were swept away by the lift. My appetite for lunch completely evaporated for a short while.

Mingling with other guests at the buffet lunch Sophie Montgomery introduced me to the Chief Executive Officer of ICAP, Mr Michael Spencer, who was hosting this extraordinary day. It was great fun meeting the other celebrities Richard Dunwoody, Lady Victoria Hervey, Anthea Turner and Barbara Windsor.

We left to go home at 3.00pm. The traders worked in shifts and it was not until the following day that I received a telephone call which astounded me. The Society had been given an incredible £100,000. What a successful day it had been.

The telephone rang in Selwyn's home one Friday afternoon in March 2003. It was a call from his contact at the Community Fund of the National Lottery announcing that BRPS had been awarded £145,257. "What good news", thought Selwyn Higgins. It would cover another three year research project led by Professor Shomi Bhattacharya at the Institute of Ophthalmology*. The project was designed to identify and study the biochemistry associated with dystrophy genes from three specific chromosomes*.

If Selwyn thought the award had brought to an end the mountain of form filling and case writing he had done when applying for this award, he was mistaken. The offer came with pages of contractual conditions, all of which had to be agreed before any payments could be made. After a few frantic days for Selwyn and George Thompson, our treasurer, the offer was formally accepted.

"Shall we apply to the Clothworkers' Foundation for some money? I'm sure it's more than five years since they stopped sponsoring our Newsletter," I asked our treasurer. The Clothworkers' Foundation has a rule that you cannot apply for further financial assistance until a period of five years has elapsed.

Early in 2005 we needed donations for the laboratory in Manchester, which is the first one in this country to receive National Health Service approval for their genotyping* of RP patients.

So it was fortuitous that the Clothworkers' Foundation was able to give us a donation of £30,000. BRPS has used it by awarding grants for this work at Manchester to be spread over five years. Although Sir Henry and Lady Jones have died their three sons and daughter remain interested in BRPS and our research programme. They have followed in their father's footsteps as members of the Clothworkers' Foundation.

The first time the Society was left a legacy I greeted the news with the words, "At last, we are established as a charity. People must really believe we will achieve our objective to find treatments if they are prepared to make us a beneficiary of their Will." The lady, who rebuked me at that first meeting of the London Branch for not wearing a hat when sitting on committees, left the Society the largest legacy it has received so far. Irrespective of the amount, large or small, it is always encouraging to be remembered in this way.

The suggestion of employing a professional fundraiser was proposed within the first year of the Society's existence. It has been discussed repeatedly over the years. I have always felt strongly that we should not risk the Society's limited funds when there is no guarantee of a good return.

How have our funds been used? To date we have allocated 185 grants to fund research projects into RP. These have totalled over seven million pounds.

So much effort has been made by our members to raise funds we should be proud of this tremendous achievement. When treatments are finally available we will be able to say ...

"We funded most of them ourselves."

Aunt Jessie

Beverley and Ben Berman

Lynda and Yasmin, 1977

Lynda and Snowy, 1991

Scottish Branch with Lynda and Irene Solomons

Chapter 7

SPREADING THE WORD
The Need for Publicity

"There's no such thing as bad publicity except your own obituary."
My Brother Brendan. Dominic Behan quoting his brother Brendan Behan 1923-1964

I had to be at Broadcasting House at 11.00am for the recording of my first interview for the 'In Touch' programme, broadcast on 11th January 1976. Only a few days beforehand I'd not even heard of the 'In Touch' programme. As I sat in the foyer of Broadcasting House waiting to be escorted to the studio, who should come through the door but Terry Wogan and Jimmy Young.

Arriving in the studio, with legs like jelly, I was settled comfortably in a chair and asked by the presenter of the programme what I'd had for breakfast. "What's that got to do with anything?" I wondered. Apparently this was for a voice level test to ensure my voice came across 'on air' smoothly.

Jane Finnis, the presenter, introduced me and asked me about the origins of the Society and why I thought it necessary to have yet another organisation for the partially sighted and blind. As I talked my nervousness ebbed away. It was a surprise to discover that the entire team of presenters for the 'In Touch' programme had a visual problem.

After the programme we went to the BBC canteen for lunch. We were surrounded by famous people whose faces I recognised. I had to refrain from jumping up to ask for autographs. I felt certain that would not be the thing to do. The weekly 'In Touch' news programme on Radio 4 addressed issues of interest to partially sighted and blind people and has given much needed publicity to BRPS. Over the years our medical advisors, research workers and members of the Management Committee have been featured on the programme.

A book entitled 'In Touch' was published on alternate years. It was written by the programme's producer, Thena Heshel OBE, and a social worker, Margaret Ford. It became the bible for anyone interested in the welfare of visually handicapped people.

I was presented with the first taped version of this book at Christ the Cornerstone church in Milton Keynes in 1993. Four members of the team for the 'In Touch' programme were there: Peter White, blind from birth, Kevin Malhern, also with a visual problem, Thena Heshel and Margaret Ford. The actress Patricia Gallimore, who plays Pat Archer on Radio 4's daily programme, 'The Archers', presented it to me. This was a double pleasure for me as I am a great fan of 'The Archers'. To celebrate the occasion a cake had been made by a completely blind lady, although I think the icing had been left to a sighted person, as it was an exact replica of the 'In Touch' Handbook.

Many years later I frequently attended Sunday evening services as well as orchestral and choral concerts in this church.

The day I first visited the office of the Royal National Institute for the Blind (RNIB) in London I met their heads of departments. "What facilities or support do you offer people diagnosed with RP?" I asked them. "Nothing specific," came the reply. I told them about our recently formed Society.

I travelled to their rehabilitation centre in Torquay. The principal, Bob Greenhaulgh, who had very little sight himself, gave us a lot of help and advice. He wrote a paper, 'RP and Mobility', which our members found helpful.

I visited all the organisations for the blind and partially sighted asking them the same question, "Could you tell me something about RP?" I wanted so much to know about this disease, but there was no material written for people without a basic knowledge of medical science.

To fill this gap our committee decided we should produce a quarterly Newsletter, which would be distributed to members, social workers, opticians and others. Articles had to be written, an editor had to be found, someone had to type it and envelopes had to be addressed. Jill Moore, John Marshall's sister, is a journalist. She agreed to edit it for the first year. An added bonus was that my Aunt Jessie had considerable experience of writing reports for her work at Harwell. She was only too pleased to write reports for us. Mary Guest contributed articles concerned with welfare, John Marshall covered the medical aspects for us and Branches were invited to send us news of their activities.

Two of my neighbours, after a little persuasion, agreed to help me with the production of the first Newsletter. Pam typed the stencils and I turned the handle of the duplicating machine with hands that became increasingly inky while Margaret typed the address labels for the envelopes. Other friends were invited to a collating party, where we all contributed to a cold buffet supper. We worked until 2.00am when we were utterly exhausted. Finally with a great sense of relief and achievement we took the bundles of envelopes to my village post office to be greeted with the words, "You've got a lot of friends."

Ann Saunders, a practising solicitor who has RP, joined our

committee as a legal advisor. She and Mary Guest became joint editors in 1977. Our current editor, Selwyn Higgins, whose wife has RP, took over the task in 1983. Since then Selwyn has written about a wide range of topics, some of which were controversial and sensitive. He has a gift of being able to write reports on medical research in language understandable to all our members. His editorials have inspired and encouraged us all.

The first edition of our Newsletter in large print appeared in January 1978. The new format was welcomed with enthusiasm, but not by me. My peripheral vision had deteriorated and I was left with a narrow tunnel of sight, as if I was looking down a gun barrel. The edge of the letters simply fell outside the tunnel.

The Newsletter was becoming increasingly difficult to produce with voluntary help. One evening Mary Guest was listening to the 'Any Questions' programme on Radio 4. On the panel that evening was Sir Campbell Adamson, the Chairman of the Confederation of British Industry (CBI). The panel was asked to describe the task they found most difficult in chairing a board meeting. Sir Campbell replied, "As I have tunnel vision I cannot see everyone at the table at once." He did not give a reason. That immediately set Mary thinking. She wrote to Sir Campbell to ask him if his tunnel vision was due to Retinitis Pigmentosa. He replied promptly expressing amazement that Mary not only knew about RP but a charity had been created to help RP sufferers. He was keen to know more about this Society and would like to meet a fellow RP sufferer.

A few weeks later I found myself in Sir Campbell Adamson's office in London, wearing a new grey velvet suit. His secretary showed me into his room. Two green sofas and a coffee table stood in front of a large, leather top desk. Coming forward to greet me he invited me to take a seat on a sofa. Coffee was brought and served in elegant white bone china cups. Soon we were exchanging our own experiences of RP.

During the Second World War he had entered the RAF to train as a pilot. His career finished before it began. On his first night exercise he was unable to find his aircraft in the dark. Consequently, due to his night blindness, he was diagnosed with Retinitis Pigmentosa.

Sir Campbell offered to assist us in any way he could. As we said good-bye he asked me if his chauffeur could take me to the railway station. I accepted his kind offer by saying, "Not to the station, but a lift to the meeting of the Management Committee would be very helpful." I felt quite disappointed, as I got out of the car, that nobody I knew was around to see me.

Soon after my meeting with Sir Campbell he was appointed Director General of the Abbey National Building Society. The next time I saw him was at their Head Office in Baker Street, London. Mary Guest came with me. We were hoping Sir Campbell would help us with our problem regarding the printing of the Newsletter. We knew Abbey National had a printing department. When Sir Campbell heard how we published our Newsletter he assured us he would arrange for it to be printed, collated and mailed by their printing department at no cost to the Society, except for postage. All we had to do was to supply addressed envelopes. Like so many large business organisations Abbey National had a fund for charitable good works. They continued doing this for us until Sir Campbell retired. Since then the Newsletter has been printed locally and the cost has been covered by sponsorship. Over the course of time the Newsletter has also been produced on cassette tape, in Braille and on compact disc.

From the start there was an urgent need to have a publicity

leaflet to inform the general public of our existence.

"I know just the person who can help you," said my Aunt Jessie. "Hugh Auger is an old family friend and owns a Public Relations company." She contacted him and after attending our committee meeting he agreed to write the first pamphlet for us.

"Do you know a child with RP whose photograph we could use in a pamphlet, provided, of course, the parents are willing?" he asked.

In those early days we did not know one family we could approach. As we drew a blank Hugh suggested reversing the roles.

"We could use a photograph of Lynda and another of her children showing how she is seeing less and less of them over time."

This was what we did and to keep down the cost the pamphlet was produced in black and white. We used this for many years until our members requested a new edition in colour.

I also wanted a booklet, giving a concise explanation of RP for our members and their families. One which was easy to understand without too many medical terms in it. It seemed to be asking for the impossible, but nothing is impossible if you try hard enough. Eventually 'A Guide to RP' was written by John Marshall and Mary Guest. This was followed by a series of booklets including, 'Your Questions Answered' (updated), 'Young People and RP', 'RP and Genetics', 'The Eye Clinic and RP', 'Mobility and Communication Skills', and 'Stem Cell Therapy'.

So often when I explained that my deteriorating eyesight was caused by RP, the response was, "Whatever's that? I've never heard of RP."

To clarify the name and aim of the Society for the general public, in 1985 the Trustees decided to follow the American RP Foundation and add FIGHTING BLINDNESS to our name of

BRPS. This practice was followed by many RP societies worldwide.

Publicity was also given to us by Janet Silver, the senior ophthalmic optician at Moorfields Eye Hospital. I visited her to see if she had a suitable low vision aid to help me with my restricted eyesight. Janet became so interested in the Society she did all she could to help us. She told all her RP patients about our existence. As a result many of them became members of BRPS. She visited a great number of our Branches to display her collection of low vision aids for the benefit of members who had no access to a low vision aid clinic. To have such an eminent person supporting the Society gave us great kudos. It was not long before she became a member of our Medical Advisory Panel.

Much later Dr Caroline Converse, our research worker at Strathclyde University, edited the RP Scientific Newsletter, which had an international circulation and was sponsored by Cantor & Silver. Research workers from around the world contributed articles about their work, acknowledging the source of their funding. Regular reference was made to BRPS by recipients of our grants for their work.

I was always on the lookout for ways of bringing the Society to the attention of the media. We wanted to target different audiences.

John Marshall and Alan Bird made a half-hour film for the Open University programme about the modes of inheritance* within RP and the characteristics of the disease. I was given a slot to advertise BRPS. It was shown on television at 5.30am.

Capital Radio had started a weekly series on health matters. Shirley Dixon wrote asking if a programme about RP would be included. Early one morning she and I arrived at the studios of Capital Radio to be interviewed by Michael Aspel. Throughout the day, on each hour following the 'News', listeners were invited to telephone a Helpline, which had been especially set up for us to answer their questions. All day long the questions kept coming. By 10.00pm we were weary and hoarse but also delighted with the promises of at least fifty new members.

Likewise three members of the Society and I answered telephone enquiries in an ITV studio following the five minute talk given by Shirley Dixon on their 'Help' programme. Local television channels also showed short 'Public Awareness' films about RP. These, too, resulted in a great response.

Andy Wiseman, the producer of the BBC programme 'Tomorrow's World', contacted me when they heard about a night vision aid developed by the International Telephone and Telegraph Corporation (ITT) at their Standard Telecommunications laboratories at Harlow in Essex.

"I can see in the dark," I cried to everyone's amazement when I looked through the device for the first time. The device resembled a monocular opera glass and worked by amplifying existing light thus enabling RP sufferers to see dark shapes and shadows through it instead of a screen of blackness.

An official presentation of the device was made to me by Lord Penny, Chairman of ITT, at a luncheon party. We lent it to Janet Silver so that she could evaluate its benefits for her RP patients. It had already completed a successful two year trial with the Swiss Helicopter Alpine Rescue Service. With the aid of this device, helicopter pilots could make night landings on glaciers in very bad weather conditions without even starlight illumination.

Andy Wiseman wanted to highlight this device in the programme, 'Tomorrow's World'. He knew nothing about RP but after a day spent with me and his team in the studio he understood the enormous potential this equipment had for people with RP. Sadly the prohibitive cost of £1,500 to the individual plus the fact that it was a cumbersome hand-held device meant it was an unrealistic proposition. It was hoped that this prototype could be adapted into a form of spectacles, but this never happened.

The producer of the BBC 'Horizon' programme exclaimed, "You don't look blind." I was being filmed with Roger Green, Chairman of our Management Committee, in the grounds where the Chelsea Annual Flower Show is held. This thirty minute programme was being made to show viewers how visual loss varies in people who have RP. At the time I still had a small amount of central vision and could see colours, whereas Roger had only peripheral vision and had lost his ability to see colours clearly. We were asked to walk along a path, lined by trees. I took Roger's arm as with his peripheral vision he was able to guide me avoiding the trees and I could see straight ahead. We were asked to read the labels at the base of the trees. Roger was unable to do this as his peripheral vision meant he could no longer see detail or read print.

I had the thrill of driving a rally car again around Silverstone Racing Circuit for a television programme. I do not advise anybody to try this unless accompanied by an experienced circuit driver with dual control. Although I was registered blind I could still read the 25-yard test, which the driving licence required. I had not driven a car for fourteen years and I was more in control of my Guide Dog than the potential killer a car is in the wrong hands. I agreed to take this car for a spin to demonstrate the inaccuracies of the eye-test at that time. Eventually a report by a House of Commons All-Party Committee was published on 16 January 1985, which called on the Ministry of Transport to re-specify the minimum visual requirements for a driving licence and to introduce regular eye-tests.

My driving career continued that year but with a different venue – this time it was Brands Hatch. Unlike Silverstone, I did not have the circuit to myself. It was disconcerting when another car passed me at 100 mph and I could not see it! Channel 4's television crew was filming me for their programme 'Well Being – Blindness', to show the general public once again that although someone is registered blind, many are fortunate enough to have some residual vision.

Members of the Society have appeared on various Radio and Television programmes. Hugo Sprinz on Radio 4's 'Farming Today' described how he managed a farm despite having RP. Carol Holmes and her Guide Dog were included in the BBC television programme, 'Songs of Praise'. Moreover RP has been used as part of story lines in television programmes such as 'Casualty' and 'Peak Practice'. Prior to the episode of 'Peak Practice' the producer arranged for a page of their website to give information concerning the disease together with details of the Society. A Helpline number appeared on the television screen at the end of the programme.

As more knowledge was gained about genetics two

programmes produced on Radio 4 were of particular interest to our members. In 1991, the renowned geneticist Dr Steven Jones gave the Reith Lecture entitled 'The Language of the Genes*'. This series helped me to understand the complexity of inherited diseases.

Years later on 16th January 2002 Radio 4 broadcast a programme 'Beyond the Genome'. Steven Jones, now a professor, together with Dr Robin Ali and Professor Shomi Bhattacharya reported on the significance of unravelling the human genome* for the future. I found it daunting to be included at the end of such a programme but it publicised the Society yet again.

Our thoughts turned to opticians and ophthalmologists. If only more of them knew about BRPS, they could spread the word of our existence among their patients. Hopefully this would increase our membership. In order to foster public awareness of the Society a series of talks to the local Branches of the British Council of Ophthalmic Opticians* and the Association of Optical Practitioners was arranged and sponsored by David Cantor. His company donated a one page advertisement in 'The Optician' magazine announcing these talks. They would be given by our medical advisors. We travelled the length and breadth of the UK covering twenty of their Branches within the year. When we attended their Oxford Congress* I spoke to many ophthalmologists about our recently launched Helpline. BRPS featured in a series of four articles in 'The Optician' magazine. We hoped that as a result all opticians would become familiar with the work of the Society.

Further efforts were made to ensure that RP became more widely known among professionals. In the year 1991-92 an article was placed in the magazine 'Doctor' which is read by 40,000 general practitioners.

In the early days of the Society press coverage was always connected to the so-called treatments. It was later that publicity came through human stories and the achievements of our members.

The magazine 'Woman's Realm' featured an article about a mother who has RP and noticed that her twelve year old son was becoming clumsier than usual. He insisted there was nothing wrong because he did not want to worry her. He even managed to keep silent when his school friends tormented him. They took him to different places, spun him around and asked him if he knew where he was. He stopped going out to play. When RP was diagnosed he quickly learnt Braille and used a Braille typewriter to take notes in class. His school friends rallied around once they understood he was going blind. They launched an appeal and raised £6,000.

We received numerous enquiries at our office following an article in the 'Woman's Own' magazine in March 1994 about my award from HM the Queen.

A similar source of recruiting new members was the medical 'Question and Answer' column in women's magazines. In 1994 an October issue of the magazine 'Bella' printed a reader's question concerning RP. The answer included the Society's address and telephone number.

BRPS collectors on street corners were yet another way of publicising the Society. When we arrived at the Grosvenor Centre in Northampton for a BRPS Flag Day Paul Skinner greeted us with the words, "We have something to help you with this street collection. Caroline has designed a tabard for collectors to wear. We've made them ourselves out of old sheets and written BRPS FIGHTING BLINDNESS on the front and back with a marker pen."

This was remarkable as Paul's wife, Caroline, had very little sight.

Caroline's design was so popular Paul explored the possibility of having tabards made professionally. We managed to obtain sponsorship from Allergan pharmaceutical company and the Abbey National Building Society.

"They ought to match the collecting boxes," suggested Paul.

They did. Brilliant yellow, PVC, multi-fitting, slipover tabards arrived at the office. Screen printed in bold black letters on the front and back of them was the Society's logo.

Fighting Blindness

Never again would BRPS collectors be unnoticed on street corners.

The Society now has its own website designed by Jonathan Abro, who has RP. Thirty years ago it was a struggle to find out anything about RP or ways of coping with it. Now simply by pressing a key on a keyboard, there is immediate access to the latest information concerning the nature of the disease, medical research into it worldwide, benefits from social services and help offered not only by our own Society but also by other related organisations.

Chapter 8

IT'S THAT TIME OF YEAR AGAIN
The AGM – A Few Memories

"The time has come ... to talk of many things."
Alice through the Looking Glass. Lewis Carroll 1832-1898

My problem was becoming a nightmare. It was my responsibility, as the Honorary Secretary of the Society, to find a hall in London, which could accommodate two hundred people without involving any cost.

Who could I turn to for ideas? I went along to the Royal National Institute for the Blind in Great Portland Street. After all, they were 'The Helping Hand for the Blind'. I was taken upstairs into the Armitage Hall. Windows, high up in the wall opposite me, let in little light. It was a hall with a high ceiling and a big organ at one end. Best of all, though, there was no charge for organisations concerned with the blind.

"This will do fine," I said.

"You'll have to put out the chairs yourselves," I was told.

"All two hundred?" I asked.

"Yes, and stack them away afterwards."

I trotted off to the Institute of Ophthalmology* and found John Marshall's technicians. "I've got a job for you." They were not perturbed by my simple request.

Since night blindness is an early symptom of RP we decided to hold our first AGM on the Saturday nearest to the longest day of the year, so that there was maximum daylight for travelling. "We've fixed the date for 25th June 1977 and found a hall. All should be plain sailing from now," I thought. Little did I realise that a lot of hard work remained to make the day a success. There was a speaker to invite, refreshments to organise, an agenda to prepare and a projector to find. Every member of the Management Committee was co-opted for a particular task.

The day dawned. A bright sunny morning. I set off with high hopes that it would mark a new and interesting era for the Society. I was excited and looking forward to meeting many new members. The only thing which marred it all was the thought of having to give a report as the Honorary Secretary. Never before had I addressed such a large audience.

I was met on the steps of the RNIB office by an official in a state of agitation. "I thought you said you were expecting no more than 150 people. There are people with RP everywhere." By two o'clock there was standing room only in the hall.

The business session over, the audience was going to hear, for the first time, an explanation of RP in terms they could understand. This was a turning-point in the history of RP. Dr John Marshall, helped by his wife Judith at the projector, showed slides of the retina and diagrams illustrating the ways in which RP is inherited. His main message, which came loud and clear, was that before thinking about treatment researchers must know what is going wrong in the eye and why.

Jessie Mole, as chairman, concluded the meeting with a challenge for the Society to fund a Research Fellowship* which would need approximately £70,000 at a British University.

"Little chance of that," I thought gloomily, as the treasurer had told us there was only £4,000 in the kitty. "It would take years." I was proved wrong.

───◆───

A year passed. It was 7.30am and the terminus at Gatwick

airport was crowded. The usual atmosphere of anticipation was everywhere. John Marshall and I were waiting for the plane to touchdown. It was bringing Ben and Beverly Berman from the American RP Foundation. They were coming with their three daughters and five other officials of the Foundation to our second AGM, which was to be held in three days' time on 24th June 1978.

I thought of all that had happened to me personally in the last twelve months. I now had my first Guide Dog, my son had survived a near fatal accident and I had moved house.

When we heard a delegation from the USA was coming to our AGM we were pleased we had found a new venue which would accommodate our numbers more comfortably. My Aunt Jessie had arranged for us to use the lecture hall at Bedford College, London University, where she had been a student. We also had the use of a second hall for our exhibitions and their beautiful gardens were open to us for picnics at lunch time.

The arrival of Ben and Beverly marked the beginning of a momentous week for the RP movement. The following day, Thursday, the ITV programme 'World in Action' went out on air showing Linda McDougall at the Opus Clinic in St Gallen, Switzerland interviewing Professor Bangerter (of chicken egg treatment fame) and some of his English patients. How controversial that programme became.

Eric Katz was one of the names Ben Berman had sent me following my visit to America in 1973. Eric was thrilled that Ben was coming to the UK and on the Friday evening he and his wife, Hazel, gave a buffet supper at their home, so that the American visitors could meet some of our Medical Advisory Board and the BRPS team. It was obvious from the murmur of voices that people were deep in conversation as they sat on the lawn that beautiful summer evening exchanging ideas. Contacts and friendships were forged which would be useful for years to come in our common fight against RP.

I did not get much sleep that night as I had to be up early the next morning in order to leave home at 7.15am, catch the train from Redhill station and cross London to Bedford College. I wanted to check everything was in place before anyone arrived. Soon I was welcoming members from Scotland, Yorkshire, Lancashire, Derbyshire, the Midlands, Wales, the West Country, London and the Home Counties. It was staggering to realise the way our network had spread in a year. There were cries of greeting as people were reunited with those they had met the previous year. Soon they were sharing their experiences of forming Branches.

A porter came bustling up to me, "The Swiss Embassy is on the telephone. They would like to speak to you."

"Whatever can this be about?" I wondered as I followed him to the telephone.

"May we have your permission for Professor Bangerter and his team, from Switzerland, to attend your meeting this afternoon?" an official at the other end of the telephone enquired. I could not believe it.

"Whatever happens," I thought, "it is imperative that he does not take over the meeting."

By this time the entrance hall and exhibition areas were crowded. At last I found John Marshall talking to Alan Bird and Geoffrey Arden.

"You'll never guess who's on his way. Bangerter."

"That should be interesting," Alan commented.

The meeting began. I welcomed the American delegation saying, "If it was not for Ben and Beverly Berman, Sally Cushner and Gordon Gund who founded the American RP Foundation, and are with us this afternoon, there would probably be no BRPS and we would not be sitting here today. We also welcome ophthalmologists* from Austria, Russia and Switzerland as well as representatives from the RP societies of New South Wales, Australia, Finland and West Germany."

The business was concluded speedily as everyone was eager to hear from our two speakers Professor Alan Laites (Chairman of the American RP Foundation's Scientific Advisory Board) and Professor Alan Bird from Moorfields Eye Hospital. They gave an overall picture of the research being carried out both in America and here in the UK. Alan Bird's talk and answers to questions were so clear and sympathetically expressed that much of what he said was met with spontaneous applause. It was during one of these outbreaks of applause I noticed Professor Bangerter leaving the hall with his team.

This memorable day was not over yet. Ben Berman concluded his talk by giving us all an open invitation to the Churchill Hotel for refreshments. Now that my responsibilities for the day had finished I could relax and chat to the people I had not been free to meet earlier. I kept well away from the table where heated discussions were going on between Bangerter and his team on the one hand and Alan Bird, Geoffrey Arden and Robert Weale on the other. During the evening I met amongst others, a young politician who had just been elected to Parliament, David Mellor. He was there with his wife, Judith, who has RP. Afterwards they took me to Victoria station where I caught the last train to Redhill. I climbed wearily into bed, knowing that the next day I had to go back up to London for the first international meeting of RP societies.

We continued holding our AGM at Bedford College for eleven

years. There were some disadvantages for our members, but the Avon Branch came to the rescue by bringing the Venture Scouts to act as guides for us. Their most popular task was exercising the Guide Dogs. One year a scout returned Isabel Yule's Guide Dog dripping wet, nobody had warned him that retrievers liked water! The lake in Regent's Park was too great a temptation.

I was waiting in the reception at Bedford College to welcome our members to the third AGM in 1979. Nobody appeared.

"What do you think has happened?" I asked Mary Guest and those who had arrived early to set up the exhibition.

At last our group from Devon turned up with the news that coaches full of police had descended on Regent's Park because of a march by demonstrators. The police had cordoned off most of the roads, including the approach road to Bedford College. Our chairman and treasurer were missing, there was no sign of the panel of speakers and as yet very few members.

Eventually a frustrated Jessie walked in having removed one of the police barricades herself. A porter took her to a telephone where she made numerous telephone calls to the Inspector in charge of the Royal Parks Police. At last he agreed that our members could be allowed through. In spite of this worrying start our audience, numbering over three hundred, was enthralled by our scientific speakers.

We rounded off the day by getting together at the Institute of Ophthalmology for a glass of wine and delicious food cooked by Judith Marshall. This began the tradition of the AGM party.

"Everything is organised. Hopefully nothing should go wrong

this year," I reassured the Management Committee a week before our fourth AGM. To my dismay five days later I heard that John Marshall, who would be chairing the medical session, had been taken seriously ill. After my initial concern for John my thoughts turned to rearranging the AGM. Alan Bird was the one person who was familiar with the research workers coming to speak from the Institute of Ophthalmology*. Fortunately I was able to get through to Alan straightaway and he readily agreed to stand in for John.

"'GET UP AND GO.' That should make our eighth AGM different from the others," I thought as I read the proposals of our Welfare Committee for the exhibition. Medical research had dominated our past exhibitions, but this year the exhibition was planned around outdoor activities and travel. We hoped this would encourage our members to find hobbies which would be suitable for them. "Together with the theme 'Eight Years and Two Breakthroughs' for the research news this should prove to be a memorable AGM," I thought. So it was. Peals of laughter echoed around the grounds of Bedford College that day as members attempted to mount tandem bicycles, shoot arrows at the target in archery and play bowls.

"I shall be approaching my 74th birthday at the next AGM," my Aunt Jessie informed me. "After twelve years it's time I retired as Chairman." This would be a wrench for me as we had worked closely together since that conversation under her apple tree in the garden at Sunningwell. However I was pleased that she intended to stay on as a Trustee. So at the thirteenth AGM in 1989 the new Chairman, Trevan Hingston, presented Jessie with a gift from the Society in gratitude for her services over the many years since the Society was formed.

"We must move out of London," I said to the members of the Management Committee. "We cannot expect our members to go on travelling hundreds of miles to the AGM." This was a proposal from the Branch Chairmen's meeting. The Coventry Branch had offered to find accommodation for us and take on the organisation of our fourteenth AGM. Thus a new pattern was set. The AGM would alternate between London and the provinces.

Hence our first AGM held out of London was presided over by our first Chairman who suffered from RP and became the occasion when the first identification of an RP gene was announced to our members. We left the meeting resolved to do all we possibly could to continue our fundraising efforts for research.

"Will I have to wear my kilt?" I asked nervously when we decided to hold our AGM in 1993 north of the border as part of the fourth Scottish Conference. All the planning was left to our Scottish members led by the Edinburgh Branch. The weekend was packed with activities, beginning with a Civic Reception on Friday evening. Dr Cliff Beevers chaired the medical and welfare sessions on Saturday.

We were all thrilled and full of admiration for Cliff. At the age of twenty he had been diagnosed with RP and was advised to leave

University on completing his first year. However he went on to gain a first class honours degree in Mathematics at Manchester University and a PhD three years later. He obtained a post in the Department of Mathematics at the Heriot-Watt College, Edinburgh University, eventually becoming a senior lecturer there. In recognition of Cliff's achievements the University was awarding him a personal Chair of Mathematics. So now it was Professor Cliff Beevers. There were great celebrations at the Dinner and Ceilidh that evening.

"I have an idea," I suggested at a meeting of the Management Committee. "The theme of the twentieth AGM should be 'BRPS THIS IS YOUR LIFE'. We'll have a Red Book. John Marshall could be Master of Ceremonies."

For our 20th anniversary we decided to hold the AGM at St Thomas' Hospital in London. Then we could organise tours, for our members, of the BRPS laboratory in the Rayne Institute during the morning. This was a challenge. The laboratory is on the fourth floor of this huge teaching hospital. Two guides, who would be wearing the Society's bright yellow tabards, would be assigned to each group of eight visually handicapped people. Keeping the group together turned out to be a difficult task for the guides as they negotiated the long, busy hospital corridors and led their party into one lift and then another.

The afternoon session with the theme 'This is Your Life' emphasised the highlights in the history of BRPS which had become an internationally known society by this time.

At the evening party, planned by Judith Marshall, a further job awaited me. To everyone's surprise there was a large birthday cake shaped as a figure 20 which was edged with the RP logo.

"Come on Lynda cut the cake," Judith called. I performed this OPERATION with a guiding hand from John who had changed from his suit into a T-shirt displaying the words, 'TRUST ME I'M A DOCTOR'.

The motorway ahead was closed. I was on the long journey to Tynemouth. "There's nothing you can do Madam but sit and wait," a policeman informed me cheerfully. "A lorry has scattered its load of microwave ovens across the carriageway."

I arrived over five hours late at the hotel for the 21st AGM of the Society as part of the Northern Conference on 6th September 1997. We had been planning it for over a year. Three of the leading research workers in the world had agreed to be the speakers: Jerry Chader (USA), Peter Humphries (Dublin) and Alan Wright (Edinburgh).

Having missed dinner that evening I was ready for breakfast the next morning and was relieved to hear all our delegates had arrived safely. However we decided to delay the start of the conference until after the funeral service of Diana, Princess of Wales.

The cost of the AGMs had concerned us for some time. "We must find sponsors," I suggested to the Management Committee.

"I'll try to find some," volunteered Sophie Montgomery.

We had reached a quarter of a century. How should we celebrate? Roger Green suggested our 25th AGM should be held in Birmingham and the Midlands Branch would be responsible for all the practical arrangements under the guidance of the

Management Committee. We set about drawing up a list of possible guest speakers who had known the Society since its beginnings. The person who came to my mind immediately was Peter White, who is the BBC Disability Affairs correspondent and the principal presenter of the Radio 4 'In Touch' programme. Although he was born blind his sole ambition, from an early age, was to become a BBC correspondent.

To represent the American Foundation we decided to send an invitation to Dr Jerry Chader who, as their Chief Scientific Officer, could give a comprehensive summary of the results from the research programmes being carried out in the USA. Another remarkable person we decided to invite was Christina Fasser. She runs the Swiss RP Society as well as being President of Retina International. Her ability to speak five languages and her command of Braille are a continual asset in this role. Although totally blind she enjoys cross-country skiing. Roger and his team set about planning the event in minute detail, including an exhibition of aids and equipment from seven organisations.

To our relief Sophie did obtain sponsorship for this AGM which enabled us to expand our plans. All was going well until I received an apologetic e-mail from Jerry Chader saying he was due for surgery and would not be fit enough to travel to our AGM. However Dr Tim Schoen would be happy to take his place. The day was a resounding success and well supported by our membership.

A significant change took place at our AGM in Bournemouth in 2003. 'FROM LABORATORY TO CLINICAL TRIALS' was the theme of this exciting day which began with a strategy meeting in the morning. We were told how the final stage towards a treatment would be planned. It would not be long before we would be genotyping* patients ready for treatment trials.

We all hope that our 30th anniversary in 2006 will bring us even nearer to our goal – a treatment and cure.

Chapter 9

HELPING HANDS
An Office, A Board of Trustees and A Management Committee

"I count myself in nothing else so happy
As in a soul, remembering my good friends."
King Richard II. William Shakespeare 1564-1616

It was 1975. I looked at the pile of letters stacked on the dining room table. No matter how hard I worked, the pile grew bigger and bigger as more and more letters arrived each day.

My girlfriends rallied round, assisting in many different ways. Ruth, Jenny, Margaret and Pam all had office skills. My close friends, Mary and Marilyn, helped by taking my children on outings to give me more time for answering these letters.

In addition to Eric Tucker I had another offer of help in response to the newspaper article in 'The Surrey Mirror'. This was from Priscilla Round-Turner. "My children are grown up, my husband works long hours in London. I have plenty of time." A wave of relief swept over me as I heard her reassuring words.

"I can re-organise the house," I thought. I persuaded the children that the conservatory would make a far superior playroom now that Helen was approaching twelve years of age. "But the roof leaks, Mummy," cried eight year old Anthony. The original playroom was transformed into an office.

We were given a filing cabinet which was delivered in style on a trailer pulled by a tractor. After I removed all the straw and gave it a good clean our first filing cabinet was installed.

"I need a desk. We can then have Sunday lunch on the dining room table once more," I said.

"I know where we can buy one really cheaply," Priscilla replied. What she didn't tell me was that it came flat packed. We drove home from Reigate with this large pack, secured with string, sticking out of the car boot.

I ached from laughing as we tried hard to assemble the desk. We thought we had finished, but it neither felt nor looked very stable. When we discovered we had missed off the feet we decided it was time to get assistance.

We set about planning our division of labour. Eric took on the typing of the Newsletter, minutes of meetings and the draft of our first booklets. Gradually Priscilla became my personal assistant. I banked all the money coming into the Society and sent details to the treasurer.

When I decided to move to nearby Redhill in 1978 I looked for a house which would have suitable accommodation for an office. The new house was a town house built on three floors. The photocopier, three further filing cabinets and the duplicating machine, all of which had been donated to the Society, were housed in the integral garage while the office was on the second floor.

The inevitable happened when Priscilla arrived one morning to tell me that she and her husband were moving to Norfolk as he was about to retire. I wondered how I would manage.

One door closed but another one opened. We had acquired a grant from the DHSS to help with our administration costs. The Trustees decided, therefore, we should employ a secretary.

"I am trying to find a part-time secretary," I told my next door neighbour. The following day there was a knock on the front door. "I understand you are looking for a secretary?" said Anne Caygill as she stood on my front doorstep. She was a secretary for a company in Redhill, but she wanted to work mornings only. She lived in the same road as me. What could be more convenient for both of us. Gentle, kind and efficient, she was our secretary for five years. I wished I could have taken her with me to Northamptonshire when my new life began with David Cantor.

Moving house is a daunting experience at the best of times, but seven days before Christmas and with little sight, preparations had to be made well in advance. "How was I to find a new secretary in time to open the office in the New Year?"

Greens Norton in Northamptonshire had a village newsletter. "I will telephone the editor," I thought.

"I'm moving to Greens Norton shortly," I told her. "I need a secretary to help me with the charity I run. Ideally I would like someone who lives in the village. May I give you a brief article describing the work of the charity and the help I need?"

"What a coincidence," came the reply. "I'm looking for a part-time job and I shall be living opposite you."

"When I come up next to finalise my moving arrangements perhaps we could meet."

It turned out that Glynis Chester had all the qualities and work experience I needed. She proved to be extremely efficient and popular with our members, and I enjoyed working with her for six years. Glynis was replaced by Belinda Gibbes, who was introduced to me by our friends who lived next door. How fortunate that I would not be without a secretary for long. Belinda quickly established a rapport with our members, but left us when she remarried three years later.

The office was becoming busier by the day. The telephone never seemed to stop ringing: calls from members, queries concerning grant applications, enquiries from social workers and other organisations. Meetings for the Board of Trustees, Management Committee, the AGM, representation at international meetings all had to be arranged. Endless paperwork was involved. Moreover by this time my ability to read print of any size had gone. Help was needed. We found a part-time assistant, Jess Pearse.

In 1992 David and I decided we needed more space, and Pond Farmhouse in Buckinghamshire seemed to meet our requirements. There were a number of outbuildings which could be converted into workshops and garages for the vintage cars. The stables could become the Society's offices, which would give us the room to expand.

Soon after the move to Pond Farmhouse I was looking for a new secretary once again. Word quickly spreads in a small village, and within a few days Kate Samwell was on the telephone. She was an experienced secretary looking for a new job and lived just one mile away. This was the start of a relationship I valued both at work and on a personal level. Kate was to share my work and support me in many different ways in the years ahead. From the beginning she was able to empathise in a sensitive way with our membership, although she had no previous involvement with visually impaired people.

When Jess left to have a baby Kate suggested that a previous colleague of hers, Yvonne Lennard, would be suitable for the part-time job. I shall always remember the times Yvonne cheered us by her witty sense of humour.

By this time the age of computers had arrived. Bob Gould transferred our membership details from the original index cards to a computer database. What an undertaking for a totally blind person. He and his wife Shirley worked at home voluntarily for thirteen years meticulously keeping these records up to date. After Bob retired from the task the database returned to the office and we employed a part-time database manager, Terry Penny, who was a retired school teacher.

For many years our Newsletter was recorded onto cassette tape in Wales by Martin and Beryl Hughes. When Martin was forced to resign as chairman of the South Wales Branch due to ill-health he asked me to find someone else to read the Newsletter.

Shortly after this, I burst into the office in great excitement. "Stop everything and listen to this," I announced.

We sat listening to a recording on cassette tape of a new format for the GDBA magazine, 'Forward'. Lively music introduced the articles read by three different people. Everyone in the office agreed it was really good.

"I could ask 'The Old Gaolers' if they would consider producing our Newsletter onto cassette tape in a similar way," Terry volunteered. 'The Old Gaolers' were the Buckingham amateur dramatic society, of which he was a keen member.

Terry found us a recording studio and each quarter four members of the 'The Old Gaolers', led by Terry, read our Newsletter onto tape. This continued for five years when Terry then decided to take a full-time job.

"I'm sure 'The Old Gaolers' will continue to read the Newsletter, but I will not be free to organise it," Terry explained.

I was having supper, a few evenings later, at the home of Hilary and Geoff Strutt, and raised the subject.

"You have a pleasant reading voice, Geoff," I said.

"What do you want?" he asked in a knowing tone.

"Terry is leaving the Society and we need someone to be responsible for producing the Newsletter onto cassette tape."

In his usual helpful way Geoff readily agreed to do this for us, despite the fact that he had taken on numerous commitments after he retired.

At the time of writing, Paul Netherton, Margaret Williams and Vivienne Eldridge, with Kate Samwell as office manager, all work part-time in the office. How thankful I am that we have such a wonderful office team working for the Society.

My own need was for a personal 'reader'. This would relieve the office staff from the time-consuming job of reading all the paperwork to me. I wrote to the Bucks Association for the Blind (BAB) asking if they knew anyone who could do this for me.

Unbeknown to me a wise, caring mother was giving her daughter some advice. "What you need to do, Hilary, is some voluntary work. It would take your mind off your own health problems. You have plenty of time as Geoff leaves early each morning."

Hilary Strutt read an article in their parish magazine in which members of the Bucks Association for the Blind were asking for volunteer drivers for blind people. She attended one of their training sessions on the day my letter arrived. The volunteers had to make a cup of coffee and prepare a light lunch while under blindfold. They quickly discovered how hard life is without sight. Hilary, who has the experience of helping a cousin, blind from RP, was asked if she was interested in becoming my reader.

She came to see me. I learnt that not only did she know about RP and Guide Dogs but she is also a qualified, practising pharmacist. Her familiarity with medical terms and her knowledge of drugs mean she has no problem reading our research grant applications or details of medical reports. Furthermore she could explain to me any medical aspects I did not understand. Reading aloud is a skill and is particularly demanding when asked to do it for any length of time. She warned me that as she suffered from an incurable physical condition, she might not be able to come every week. That was in July 1992 and Hilary has never missed our Friday afternoon reading session.

Another one of Hilary's talents is her accomplished piano playing. She and her husband, Geoff, are enthusiastic music lovers and attend local concerts regularly. After David and I separated they invited me to join them on their visits to the theatre.

When I moved from Pond Farmhouse in 2001 we found offices for the Society to rent in Buckingham. Consequently I was no longer in the office on a daily basis. Kate took on the additional responsibilities efficiently, keeping in regular contact with me by telephone.

Hilary and Geoff took me to see a house in Stony Stratford. Hilary guided me around each room, carefully describing the layout. After a second visit I decided it was a suitable location. The easy part was buying the house, especially as my daughter Helen, who was by now a solicitor, arranged all the legal transactions. The move was a huge undertaking and I could not have managed without the help of Hilary and Geoff. Every room had to be re-decorated and curtains chosen. How I came to appreciate Hilary's gift for interior design.

Since 1997 Hilary has escorted and guided me on numerous occasions to the London meetings and functions connected with the Society while Geoff has accompanied us elsewhere in this country and abroad, sometimes making it a holiday for us all.

On the one hundredth birthday of Hilary's mother in 2003 I thanked her for the good advice she had given her daughter. She could not have foreseen all that Hilary would do for me, and what a true friend she has become.

In the autumn of 1976, as a registered charity, we had written into the Deed of Trust that the eight founder members would be appointed Trustees of the Society. We called our first meeting as a Board of Trustees in November that year. Our first task was to select officers from among us.

"You're the obvious person to be our Chairman, Harry," Jessie declared.

Harry Carlisle was not so sure.

"I think the Chairman of this Society should either have RP himself or have a close relative with the disease," he replied.

"Harry, we do not have such a person at the moment," I said, "But as soon as I find someone who fulfils the criteria we'll think about it again."

After some persuasion from us all he reluctantly agreed to become a temporary Chairman.

"I'll take the post of Treasurer," Jessie volunteered.

There was a consensus of opinion that I should be the Honorary Secretary.

"I'll cover welfare," Mary Guest offered enthusiastically.

"John, you will become Chairman of our Medical Advisory Board, won't you?" I nervously asked John Marshall.

Alan Wells took on publicity and James Hudson publications. No-one would receive any remuneration. Now the Board was established our hope was that the Society would always be led either by RP sufferers or their family members.

"I am a caretaker Chairman. You do understand that Lynda," Harry Carlisle reminded me yet again. So I was pleased when Eric Katz showed an interest in the way the Society was developing. I had written to him along with the other people whose names Ben Berman had sent me after my first visit to America. In spite of his advanced RP Eric had achieved outstanding success in the business world. In his early twenties, having been diagnosed with RP, he obtained a job working on the factory floor of a glass manufacturer. After learning all he could about the processes involved he set up his own business producing glass laboratory equipment and founded Epsom Glass Industries. With his business acumen Eric became a great asset as a Trustee. It was not long before he succeeded Harry Carlisle as Chairman. For seven years his wise counsel and quiet manner steered us through our meetings.

"I've found my replacement for you," said Eric Katz trying to reassure me when he resigned as Chairman. Like Eric, Trevan Hingston was diagnosed with RP in his twenties. He travelled the world throughout his working life on behalf of Shell International and before his retirement was a senior consultant in the huge Royal Dutch/Shell Group. He carried his energy and enthusiasm into his work as our Chairman, but after eight years he was forced to retire due to ill health.

Our next Chairman, Dr Alan Rudge (now Sir Alan) retired as Deputy Chief Executive of British Telecommunications in 1997. Today he serves on a number of national and international advisory committees and brings to BRPS considerable high level management skills. A long-standing member he became a Trustee in 1992. His only daughter has Usher Syndrome*.

"Professor James Crews has always been active in the Society. I would like to ask him if he would be willing to become a Trustee," John Marshall proposed soon after the Board of Trustees was established.

"It would be beneficial to have a clinician whose work brings him into daily contact with patients in a busy Hospital Eye Department."

As a research scientist John's work is laboratory based. How pleased we were when James accepted. He was the Senior Consultant Ophthalmologist* at the Birmingham and Midland Eye Hospital where he had worked since 1959. Together with Dr Sarah Bundy he set up the Genetic Eye Clinic* there. He realised the value of our Society for his patients and served as a Trustee until 1992 when serious illness forced his resignation.

Before resigning James recommended that Alistair Fielder, who had worked with him at the Genetic Ophthalmic Clinic in Birmingham, should succeed him as a Trustee. James introduced me to Alistair soon afterwards when we had lunch together in Birmingham.

"I have always followed the activities of BRPS with interest," Alistair told me that day. "I know John Marshall. I work with him on committees of two other organisations who give grants for medical research into eye conditions. My clinical and research interests, though, have been focused mainly on matters relating to the eyesight of children."

James Crews died in 1994. The news was received with great sadness by his friends, colleagues and those who owed so much to his knowledge and skill. He was kind, compassionate and cared deeply about the suffering of others.

An idea came to me as I sat next to Sarah Bundy at the funeral service for James in St George's Church, Edgbaston. The Society should recognise the exceptional contribution James had made.

"It would be appropriate to have a student fellowship named after James," I whispered to Sarah.

"That's a wonderful idea," she said.

This confirmation convinced me it was the right thing to do. Sarah had worked with James for more than twenty years. Their Genetic Eye Clinic at the Birmingham and Midland Eye Hospital was one of the first in the UK. She was a highly respected and original researcher who enthused and trained many young doctors and scientists.

At the next meeting of the Board of Trustees I put this proposal forward. They agreed unanimously. All we had to do was raise £60,000.

When I told Annie, James' wife, she was thrilled.

"I would like to make the first donation," she said. "I didn't know what to do with James' ophthalmic instruments. They can be sold and the proceeds given to the fund."

The fundraising team worked hard. In 1997 'The James Crews Memorial Studentship' amounting to £67,345 was awarded for a project led by Dr M Seabra at Imperial College, London over a period of three years.

A year after James' death we were delighted to hear that Alistair Fielder had become the first Professor of Ophthalmology at Imperial College, School of Medicine, London. He served as a Trustee for nine years scrutinising the grant applications with John Marshall and visiting many Branches as a medical speaker. I will always remember his support as we faced difficult issues.

When Alistair Fielder indicated he would like to resign as a Trustee in 2001 due to his increasing workload, I was pleased that Professor Anthony Moore agreed to replace him.

I remembered the first time I met Tony Moore in 1988 after sitting nervously in the waiting room of the Eye Department at Addenbrookes Hospital, Cambridge. The day before an optician had told David that he thought I had a growth in my left eye. As if it wasn't bad enough having RP. After a thorough examination Tony Moore reassured me that there was nothing to worry about.

My next visit to his clinic was with my daughter, Helen.

"Mummy, I've had a car accident," she had sobbed down the telephone. It wasn't as bad as it sounded, for she was not hurt. The car had a nasty dent, but it was her words which had disturbed me. She kept saying, "I didn't see the car." A dreadful fear had crept over me. She was the same age as I was when I reversed into my neighbour's car. It took all my courage to ask, "Should we have your eyes examined?"

We arranged an appointment with Tony Moore. It was such a relief to hear Tony's words. "There's no sign of RP Helen."

"I expect it was a momentary lack of concentration," I added.

Therefore my experiences as a patient of Tony's gave me great confidence in him. He is involved in both the clinical and research aspects of RP at Addenbrookes Hospital, Cambridge and at Moorfields Hospital where he works closely with Alan Bird.

"There are too many people on this Management Committee. It's becoming unruly," I exclaimed. In the early years we accepted gladly anyone who offered their services and had expertise in a particular field. Sitting around the table were four elected members and four co-opted members of the Management Committee, in addition to eight Trustees, making a total of sixteen people. The original committee had decided in 1975 to call themselves the Management Committee. As soon as we had a

Board of Trustees they were invited to attend Management Committee meetings. Hence the present situation.

Jessie had chaired our meetings of the Management Committee until her retirement in 1989. Eric Twelves, whose wife has RP, took on this role for the next six years. He was a retired bank manager and had aided Jessie in writing the rules for the Branches. He never became ruffled and chaired our meetings in a calm and businesslike way. When he retired in 1995 a new Chairman had to be found.

"Roger, would you consider taking over from Eric?" I asked tentatively.

"I must think about that and discuss it with Margaret," Roger Green replied.

I knew Roger would not take on such a demanding and responsible position lightly, but he had experience within the Society to bring to the role of chairing the Management Committee. He and Margaret had felt inspired at the first AGM to start a Midlands Branch. A Branch which continues to thrive to this day, with perhaps a hundred members attending their monthly meetings. He also became Chairman of the Branch Chairmen's Meetings.

"If I can find someone to replace me as Chairman of the Midlands Branch I will chair the Management Committee for two years," Roger told me.

More than ten years later he continues to hold this position.

Roger had worked for British Leyland until he took early retirement when he finally lost all his sight. When he and Margaret are not visiting their grandchildren, Roger can be seen walking his Guide Dog or on the back of a tandem bicycle riding with a friend, sometimes covering ninety miles a day.

A major project lay ahead. Both the Management Committee and the Trustees agreed we needed to look at the ways the Society operated. A steering committee, led by Roger Green, was appointed to set out a practical 'Way Forward' which would allow BRPS to attain its objectives in the most efficient manner. Almost every month we met as the steering committee at my house. The other four members travelled long distances by road or rail. We spent a full day studying and discussing the structure and methods of working within the Society before they embarked on the long journey home.

Our final recommendations were agreed by the Board of Trustees and the Management Committee in 1997 and were written up in a document entitled 'The Way Forward'. This clarified the difference between the responsibilities of the Board of Trustees and the Management Committee. They were to meet separately.

The Board of Trustees should be responsible for the overall structure and strategies of the Society and all financial matters. This includes awarding grants for medical research. An application for a grant is circularised among the Trustees and sent to three independent referees, chosen from among the Society's eminent medical and research advisors for their special knowledge and expertise in that particular field. The reports of these referees are considered at a meeting of the Board of Trustees when a vote is taken on whether to award the grant. It is my job to write to each applicant. For those who are successful the award is offered with terms and conditions including an annual review of their work by the referees.

The Management Committee should be responsible for the day-to-day running of the Society. It would be comprised of seven managers who would cover Welfare, Public Relations, Publications, Fundraising, Branch Affairs, International

Representation and the Website.

Although writing 'The Way Forward' was a lot of work it has streamlined the organisation and function of the Society in the 21st century. It has also made me realise how far we have come and how much we have achieved since that first committee meeting in August 1975.

Chapter 10

WHO WILL LISTEN?
Welfare and the Helpline

"I get by with a little help from my friends."
John Lennon and Paul McCartney 1967

"How can I best help all these people who telephone me?" I asked the Management Committee.

Remembering my own thirst for knowledge about RP, my desire for some understanding of the implications and my need for guidance at the time I was first diagnosed, I was anxious to give my undivided attention to these callers.

"An answerphone would be one solution," suggested one committee member.

"That would mean I could call them back when I was free to listen to them, certainly," I said.

I had not foreseen the number of telephone calls I would receive. Gladly I had allowed my home telephone number to be printed on our letterheads, in the Newsletter and on all our leaflets. Calls were coming incessantly at all times of the day. I could be boiling eggs for breakfast, hanging out the washing, bathing the children or reading them a bedtime story.

"But, it would be very expensive," I continued. Not many homes had an answerphone in the 1970s.

"We could try to persuade someone to donate it. After all our first typewriter and filing cabinets were donated," another committee member hastened to add.

The local Rotary club was pleased to help us before the school summer holidays began. Most of the calls were from RP sufferers about a range of problems they were facing. What were the different types of RP? Would their children inherit the disease? Should they stop driving? When should they start using a white cane? These were some of the most common questions I was asked.

Thankfully Mary Guest had a keen interest in caring for the well-being of people with RP, especially those with the additional problem of a hearing loss. Together we compiled a questionnaire endeavouring to assess the need for information and support among our members. This formed the basis of our future welfare policy.

Others were also concerned about the welfare of those suffering with RP. They soon linked up with Mary to form a Welfare Panel comprising of Elizabeth Baio (Worcester), Jessica Finch (Cambridge), Margaret Green and Bob Gould (Birmingham), Eva Scarrott (Cumbria) and Irene Solomons (Glasgow). Their professional skills combined with their personal experience of RP proved invaluable in advising and supporting our members. I learnt a great deal from them. They met for their first meeting in December 1982 at the home of Bob Gould in Birmingham. Mary became the Society's Welfare Secretary, handing over the editorship of the Newsletter to Selwyn Higgins.

During her five years as Welfare Secretary Mary developed her work with those people who have the dual handicap of RP and a hearing loss, known as Usher Syndrome*. In October 1985 she organised the first meeting for parents of children with Usher Syndrome. This was followed by residential weekends for them. By 1987 her involvement with this group had grown to such an extent that she could no longer continue as our Welfare Secretary. Bob Gould replaced her.

He was already familiar with the members of our Society

through his work on the database, and his unique quality of caring for others came across as he sought to help people with their problems. He had been forced to retire early from his full-time employment due to his loss of sight and was pleased to take on a new challenging project.

―◆―

I know only too well that acquired visual loss is hard for a person to come to terms with. Almost without exception people go through the emotional stages of shock and depression before accepting their condition. Some people who lose their vision because of a degenerative process have more difficulty in accepting their condition than those who suddenly become totally blind. We all feel that 'whilst there is light there is hope'.

The Welfare Panel, with their positive attitude towards coping with RP, placed great importance on each welfare issue that arose. To help cover some of these issues our series of booklets were published. The Panel also set out to link those needing help through a difficult period in their lives with other organisations who had the relevant expertise. Often people were seeking advice regarding application for statutory benefits and services whether at home, at work, for leisure pursuits or when travelling. An example which has enabled me to operate the washing machine, cooker and microwave was explained to me by a social worker. She arrived with a tube similar to toothpaste – called High Markers. She proceeded to mark the temperatures I most frequently used with a raised dot from the tube. This was left to harden for twenty-four hours. It has given me much more independence.

―◆―

"I think it's important to encourage each Branch to identify their own Welfare Officer from among their members," Bob Gould proposed to the Management Committee.

We all agreed that was an excellent plan. Every Branch would then have someone who was known personally to their Branch members and at the same time was familiar with the local services and amenities. These Branch Welfare Officers would also be a point of contact for the Welfare Panel to pass on updated information concerning welfare matters.

Residential weekend conferences were planned by Bob and Shirley Gould to prepare these Branch Welfare Officers for their responsibilities. They were held in Sheffield with the dual purpose of sharing information with each other as well as learning from speakers and fostering mutual support. They were opportunities for getting to know each other in a relaxed and informal way.

Bob and I felt strongly that what we really needed was a Helpline which would operate in the evenings from Monday to Friday. When we moved the office to Northamptonshire our first telephone line dedicated to the Society was installed. The 50+ Club in the village invited me to speak to them about RP. In my talk I told them that I intended to start a Helpline for our members, but I needed some volunteers to take the evening calls. After the question and answer session following my talk several people offered their services for this new venture. Members from the Welfare Panel came to meet them. They gave them guidance and advice on how to respond to the enquiries they were likely to be asked.

We were now ready for an official opening of our new Helpline. We needed a celebrity. My husband, David, whose company manufactures contact lenses, had met the actor Tom Watt who was playing Lofty in the television programme 'EastEnders'. Tom was about to leave the cast to begin acting in a West End production. For his new part he was required to replace his glasses with contact lenses, and David helped him. Tom was only too willing to launch the Society's Helpline.

Once we had agreed a date with Tom, 10th April 1987, David sent out a press release to both national and local newspapers. I organised a buffet supper to which we invited the 50+ Club and the Society's Welfare Panel. Tom answered the first telephone call that evening: "This is Lofty of 'EastEnders' speaking. I am pleased to tell you that you are the first person to use the new Helpline of the BRPS."

We set up a fortnightly rota for the volunteers from the 50+ Club. As company for each other two of them would be in the office from 6.00pm until 10.00pm to answer any in-coming calls. They always brought something with them to do in any spare time, whether it was the game Scrabble, tapestry work, knitting or calligraphy.

The success of 'The Week's Good Cause' appeal on Radio 4 by Rabbi Lionel Blue had given us the financial confidence to proceed with the Helpline. The final total of £24,000 was the fifth largest amount raised by this programme for that year. The interest paid on this capital has contributed towards the running costs of the Helpline ever since.

What a wonderful start for the Helpline the members of the 50+ Club gave us throughout that summer of 1987. As we approached the long dark winter evenings Bob suggested we shared the five evenings between five members of the Welfare Panel.

"How do we do that?" I asked. "They live in different areas of the country."

"It's simple," replied Bob. "Each evening you put onto your answering machine the name and telephone number of the person to contact."

This system worked well until the number of calls during office hours made it imperative that we install a separate Helpline in 1999. What a wonder modern technology is. The telecommunications service diverted calls automatically to the Helpline operator on duty. Twelve additional volunteers, co-ordinated by Steve Goulden, meant the Helpline could be extended to cover weekdays from 9.30am until 9.30pm. Callers could leave their name and telephone number on an answering service at any time the Helpline was not operating.

To ensure that no one would be deterred from seeking help by the cost of calls, in January 2004 we introduced a local call rate on our Helpline number 0845 123 2354. This number was well publicised in our Newsletter and leaflets. In addition a small card, the size of a business card, was sent to hospitals for distribution among patients.

We felt that it was essential to arrange some training for the team of volunteers operating the Helpline.

"We have two experienced social workers on our Welfare Panel: Hilary Davies and Barbara Norton. They both have RP and are qualified to plan a programme of training," Anne Fisher informed us.

Anne had succeeded Bob as Welfare Manager the previous year. A mother of two boys who have RP, she had worked closely with Bob on the Welfare Panel for many years. A residential weekend was held at Exhall Grange School for visually handicapped children in the year 2000.

There are certain moments in your life you never forget. Diagnosis of RP was one such moment for me.

"Would you have found it helpful to talk to someone with RP at that time?" Mary Guest asked me.

"If only …" I sighed.

"I am going to propose to the Trustees that we ask Alan Bird if he would consider having Barbara Norton in his retinal diagnostic clinic*," Mary continued.

Neither of us foresaw the amount of red tape there would be before this was achieved. Eventually in 1991 Barbara began attending the clinic to give guidance and support to newly diagnosed and other sufferers of RP. Such was Barbara's success at Moorfields Eye Hospital that two years later she and Alan Bird were interviewed on the Radio 4 'In Touch' programme about her work there. Today Barbara and her Guide Dog are well known at the clinic.

Three years later Hilary Davies carried out similar counselling work at the Western Infirmary in Glasgow.

When parents are confronted with the news that their child has RP they tend to go through a series of emotions. Often disbelief soon turns to despair. One such mother in her desperation telephoned our Helpline. Susie Radford wanted to talk to other parents in the same situation and enquired if we had a Parent-Link Group.

I took her call, replying, "No, we haven't. It could be helpful, though. Why don't you write a short article for the Newsletter inviting other parents to contact you with a view to establishing such a group?"

This led to the start of a telephone link between parents.

While the Society is careful not to duplicate what is offered by other voluntary bodies or the State in terms of welfare, we always endeavour to listen to our members' problems, however large or small. It is easy to add up the money we've raised for our medical research grants but the time our members give to supporting each other is priceless.

Launching the appeal for the Rayne Institute at the B.T. Tower, 1992
Left to right: Prof John Marshall, Trevan Hingston, Lynda, David Cantor, Sir Campbell Adamson and Sir Alan Rudge

AGM 1986, Lynda and Eric Katz OBE

20th Anniversary AGM
Left to right: Mary Guest, Prof John Marshall and Lynda

Management Committee, February 2006
Left to right, back row: Lynda, Selwyn Higgins, Mireille Portlock, Stephen Jones, Alan Foster, Clive Fisher and Jonathan Abro
Left to right, front row: Linda and Colin McArthur, Anne Fisher, Brian Lay and Roger Green

Lynda and Tom Watt inaugurate the Helpline, April 1987

David, Lynda, Helen and Anthony after the Investiture, February 1994

Chapter 11

BEYOND THESE SHORES
Retina International

"Union is strength."
Mid 17th century proverb

"We have a visitor coming today from Germany," I told the children over breakfast in the summer of 1977. "I would like you to speak clearly and slowly at teatime."

When Dr Rainald von Gizycki arrived he spoke perfect English. I was slightly embarrassed, when the children came in for tea and greeted him by slowly emphasising each word.

"G-O-O-D A-F-T-E-R-N-O-O-N."

"I-T-'S N-I-C-E T-O M-E-E-T Y-O-U."

Rainald is not a medical man, but he has RP and was planning to form a German RP Society. He had heard about the British Society and was eager to learn how I had started. He had been in touch already with the Finnish Society.

I had heard from Ben Berman in America that there were RP Societies also starting in Australia and Canada. "Was this the beginning of a worldwide RP movement?" I wondered.

"London has been chosen as the venue for the first meeting of the International Association of Retinitis Pigmentosa Societies," Dr John Marshall informed our committee in April 1978. "We could run it in conjunction with our own AGM."

So as well as organising our own second AGM we would be co-ordinating the first international meeting. Everything fell into place.

Soon after dawn on Sunday 25th June 1978 I was up early to enjoy another full day. The previous Wednesday I had met the American party at Gatwick. On Friday I had been at the supper party in the home of Eric and Hazel Katz and had a busy day on Saturday with our AGM followed by the evening reception.

I set off for London once more that Sunday morning, arriving at the Churchill Hotel in good time for a 9.00am start of the first international meeting. It was an impressive sight. The room was arranged formally with a top table and side arms. The national flag of each country represented stood on a little stand, by the allocated places. As the hosts the Americans were on the top table. In addition to us there were delegates from New South Wales, Australia, Finland, West Germany, Austria and Israel. Each country gave us a progress report of their plans for the creation or growth of their Society. Then the meeting defined the aims of an international association. We decided the purpose of such an association was to co-ordinate the medical research on RP, to support national RP associations and establish through them an effective chain of communication. An immediate outcome was to set up an international Scientific Advisory Committee. Professors Geoffrey Arden, Alan Bird, Barrie Jay and Dr John Marshall were to represent the UK.

Our final function was lunch at Moorfields Eye Hospital followed by a conducted tour and later at the Institute of Ophthalmology* to see the research that was underway. Another important step forward had been made by founding the International Retinitis Pigmentosa Association (IRPA).

"The brochure for the American Congress in Baltimore has arrived Anne. It's entitled 'A DECADE TOWARDS DISCOVERY'." This was to celebrate the tenth anniversary of the American RP Foundation and include the second international meeting of IRPA. Anne, my secretary, and I pored over the contents.

"Whew! This is a smart folder," I exclaimed. "What an agenda. Just look at all these medical research scientists and ophthalmologists* scheduled to speak on the first day. I've never been at a gathering of so many before. And the whole of the next day is given to Human Sciences, which is the same as our Welfare. Nineteen one and a half hour sessions. How will they manage that? Oh, it's all right they are divided into four sets running concurrently."

"Look, here's your name on the panel of speakers for one of the sessions," Anne pointed out.

I had not realised how big this Congress would be when Ben Berman asked me to join the panel on 'Mobility and Maintaining an Independent Life Style'. There was no turning back now, though.

"The overseas delegates are invited to arrive a day early for the second business meeting of IRPA," I explained to Anne. "We have a busy time ahead making all the arrangements. First we must find out who is likely to come. Then I must check my passport, apply for a visa and make arrangements for Helen, Anthony and Yasmin."

John F Kennedy airport was crowded when I arrived in America on my own for the Congress. In 1981 Guide Dogs were not allowed to accompany their owner on flights to America and I was reliant on my white cane. When people see a Guide Dog approaching them they naturally step aside to make a pathway. A white cane does not have the same impact. A voice came over the tannoy. "British passport holders over here, please."

"Over where?" Anxiously I asked the person next to me.

Soon I was being guided by a helpful fellow traveller through customs to the arrival lounge. A sense of relief swept over me as I heard my name. There was Susie waiting for me. I would be staying with her for a week in her lovely Connecticut house before going to Baltimore for the second international meeting of IRPA.

Helena and Matt Viitasaari from Finland met me at New York Grand Central railway station so that we could travel to Baltimore together. Arriving at the Hyatt Hotel I felt I had been transported into another world. This huge brand new futuristic hotel, with its glass lifts and gleaming stainless steel, overlooking the harbour was the setting for our IRPA Congress. Ben Berman had negotiated a low rate for us with the hotel management.

Aunt Jessie, with whom I was sharing a room, and Mary Guest were waiting for me in reception. They had familiarised themselves with the hotel. As I unpacked Jessie told me she had seen many of the overseas visitors already and we would be meeting them for dinner.

Our horizons were widening. Jerome Cardin, as chairman, welcomed four new member countries, Canada, South Africa, Switzerland and Western Australia, at the business meeting of IRPA early the next morning. We were looking forward to hearing news from all the other countries before we debated our aims and objectives. As vice-chairman of IRPA Eric Katz took over in the afternoon. Setting up a worldwide organisation was far more complicated than any of us had imagined. Nevertheless we were all optimistic that it would be achieved.

The audience grew in vast numbers as we were joined the following day by more members of the American Foundation for the beginning of the Congress. The programme for the entire day was taken up by reports of medical research worldwide. Surely with this amount of effort by so many highly qualified scientists there would be a breakthrough soon.

Finally we all found the last day helpful in many practical ways regarding life skills. We, the audience, were trying to cope with RP. This was an opportunity to learn from each other.

Thus a pattern for our international meetings was established. The host country would co-ordinate a three day meeting. The first day would become a meeting of the General Assembly, eventually made up of two representatives from each member country. Scientists from all over the world would report on their work on the second day. Workshops on welfare issues would feature on the last day. These international congresses would take place every other year in the future.

Returning home I landed at Gatwick airport on the morning of my fortieth birthday. The Congress at Baltimore had broadened my vision for BRPS. I had seen how the Charity, which had started as a small struggling group of dedicated people, could have a major influence on the development of the RP movement worldwide. What an inspiring experience the Congress had been.

I took to the skies again in 1983 when Yasmin and I flew to visit our newly formed Northern Ireland Branch. I arrived in torrential rain. Bill Foster, the Chairman, and his wife drove me through a cloudburst to meet Professor Desmond Archer, a member of our Medical Advisory Board. He was a consultant ophthalmologist* at the Royal Victoria Hospital in Belfast and was very supportive of the Branch.

After our lunch together we set off to the television studios to pre-record an interview to be shown on the regional news later in the evening.

Despite the continuing dreadful weather, members from all over the Province travelled to the Branch meeting that evening where they gave me a warm welcome. They wanted to hear how the Society had started and how it was growing from strength to strength.

A different experience awaited me the following morning as I journeyed by train from Belfast to Dublin. We stopped at the border for routine checks by two British soldiers who wanted to know why I was travelling to Dublin.

I had spoken to Michael Griffith on numerous occasions by telephone as he planned to begin a Republic of Ireland Branch of BRPS. Now I was to meet him.

"As this is to be our first public meeting, I've booked the ballroom at the Royal Dublin Hotel," Michael explained to me.

"How many people are you expecting then?" I asked.

"More than a hundred I hope."

I was flabbergasted. I had anticipated a dozen people meeting in someone's sitting room. The response more than fulfilled Michael's wildest dreams. Some people had travelled long distances, many had never met anyone else with RP and all were impatient for information. I told my story once again with the added emphasis of the international meeting in Baltimore.

"RP is a worldwide condition," I told them.

At the end of the meeting Michael confided in us. "We have a problem. We now have to pay for the hire of this grand room."

Hastily bread baskets were found and passed around for donations. Needless to say there was more than enough to cover all the expenses. It was not long before they became an independent Society with Michael taking an active part in IRPA.

On 17th May 1984 Michael Griffith arranged to meet the British delegation at Heathrow airport ready to fly to the third IRPA Congress in Helsinki. David and I arrived early at the airport. We soon found John and Judith Marshall and Aunt Jessie. We checked in our luggage and were waiting to go through customs. Still there was no sign of Michael. At last, with little time to spare, Michael appeared through the crowds.

"I've left my passport at home," he announced. "You go on. I'll sort it out."

Fortunately the Irish Embassy in London issued him with a temporary passport enabling him to catch a later flight that day.

I was glad to see Helena Viitasaari, waiting to welcome me in the reception of the hotel. She was co-ordinating this Congress. I had not seen Helena and Matt since we were at Baltimore together. Neither had I seen Ben and Beverly Berman. More and more people arrived. This time there were representatives from ten member countries.

That evening there was a knock on our bedroom door. Shomi Bhattacharya, John and Judith Marshall asked if they could come in. All three were beaming from ear to ear.

"We've some really good news. Shomi's work is going to be published in NATURE."

This is the Journal in which significant scientific advancements are published. A few of us knew that Shomi and Alan Wright had discovered a marker* indicating the position of an RP gene*. Now the entire medical world would know. An elated Shomi, sitting on the edge of the bed, was soon on the telephone to Alan in Edinburgh.

"We must have a drink to celebrate this great news," David suggested.

All I could muster were two miniature bottles of schnapps that had been left in the room to welcome us. Amid much laughter I served the schnapps in tooth mugs. There was another knock at the door. "Am I missing a party?" my aunt enquired.

"If you fetch your tooth mug you can listen to the wonderful news."

We were so proud that a British team had achieved this breakthrough.

We had to come down to earth with a bump the next morning for the IRPA business meeting chaired by Ben Berman. Both Jerome Cardin and Eric Katz had resigned due to other commitments. To my surprise I was elected to succeed Eric as vice-chairman.

Some eighty people attended throughout the Congress but on the final day the audience was augmented by about two hundred members of the Finnish Society. They came from all parts of Finland to hear the reports and discussion on research topics. When the audience learnt of Shomi's achievement he received a standing ovation. Here was the first scientific breakthrough in the search for an RP gene and hopefully an eventual treatment.

By the time the fourth IRPA Congress took place in Bad Nauheim, West Germany in 1986 there were twenty-one member countries with five hundred attendees. With the growth of so many RP societies research was now beginning in several other European countries. Seven of our own researchers participated in the scientific sessions.

To encourage the countries in the Asian-Pacific region the next

Congress of IRPA was held in Melbourne, Australia. Although David and I decided not to go, the UK was well represented by a sizeable number of people, who decided to make it part of their annual holiday. They were glad to leave behind the dreary grey days of November for the warmth of an Australian summer.

Sadly Ben Berman had resigned as President of IRPA for health reasons. Aunt Jessie and Trevan Hingston represented the UK at the meeting of the General Assembly when Dr Rainald von Gizycki from West Germany was elected as the new President.

The Scientific Advisory Committee was replaced by a Scientific Advisory Board (SAB). John Marshall and Alan Laties became co-chairmen and representation was invited from every national society's medical board. This was good news for the cause of RP. It meant that the SAB could maintain oversight of RP research worldwide, preventing duplication and speeding the progress. Moreover scientists would exchange ideas informally in the bar or lounge at these gatherings.

"The Irish Sea should be calm in July," I thought. Having had the experience of a rough crossing I was a little dubious about our trip to the sixth IRPA Congress in Dublin in 1990. We would be driving through the Welsh mountains to Holyhead to board the ferry to Dublin. Everything was organised and the car was packed, when I had a message from Pat, the wife of Trevan Hingston. He had been admitted to hospital with chest pains and had to undergo surgery immediately. Apart from being the other UK delegate at the meeting of the General Assembly, Trevan was to chair several sessions and workshops throughout the Congress.

'COOPERATION AND COORDINATION CAN CURE', was the

theme of this Congress in the beautiful setting of Trinity College, Dublin. I will always remember this Congress for the four major announcements in the scientific sessions, combined with a magnificent social programme and the distinguished Irish dignitaries who were present.

Arriving at the hotel we found there was limited car parking space and we were forced to leave our car in the road. In spite of showing my disabled badge to the doorman he could not find us a space; consequently we were running late for the reception at the Mansion House that evening. In the splendour of the rooms at the Mansion House, with their plush carpets and priceless paintings, we renewed our contacts with representatives from all parts of the globe. David went to look for Michael Griffith amongst the crowds to find out if he knew about Trevan. Over dinner we re-arranged the programme, suggesting people who could cover for Trevan.

Another unexpected turn of events came when Michael casually announced, "Lynda, I hope you don't mind, but I've arranged for you to be interviewed on the Gerry Ryan chat show tomorrow morning quite early."

"How early?"

"They would like you to be at the radio studio by 7.00am if possible," he replied smiling.

On our return to the hotel from the radio studios the next day the doorman greeted us, "It was you on the Gerry Ryan show just now wasn't it?"

From then on we were allocated a parking space at the front of the hotel with a notice which stated, 'RESERVED: VIP!'

By the time the first day was over it was a pleasure to enjoy an early evening drink at Dublin Castle which had been opened especially for everyone attending the Congress.

On the Scientific day it was exciting to hear about the recent success in the research work. Professor Ropers in Holland, partially funded by BRPS, had identified*, isolated*, cloned* and sequenced* the gene for choroideremia*. A group from the USA gave us news of the Usher type 2 gene*. Shomi updated us on his progress with the autosomal dominant type* and finally we heard about the dietary treatment for Gyrate Atrophy*.

With all this good news we set off in high spirits to relax at the famous Jury's Hotel for a cabaret and dinner. The climax of these social events was the Gala Dinner on the final evening when I had the privilege of being taken into dinner by His Excellency Dr Patrick Hillery, the President of Ireland. It seemed only hours before that the Congress had been opened by Mr Noel Treacy, Minister of State at the Department of Health.

I have visited many countries, but my memories of Malta remain vivid to this day. This small island, steeped in history, and its people fascinated me each time I went there.

Although these were welcome holidays for me they were business trips for David, who knew all seven ophthalmologists* and most of the opticians* on the island. We shared many social occasions together in their homes. It was at one such dinner party that a chance remark was made to me.

"We have a number of RP patients on Malta, there ought to be an organisation like yours for them." This started me thinking.

The next time I went to Malta I suggested to one of the opticians, who was well-known on the island,

"Why don't you contact all the RP patients here and ask them if they would like a Maltese RP Society? If so, I will ask Professor John Marshall to come and talk to them."

Thus in 1993 John and Judith joined us for a full weekend in

Malta. A series of meetings had been planned. First, a pleasant social evening for John to meet our hosts in the 'Silent City' which was a favourite haunt of ours. We loved the tranquillity of this walled city of Medina where motor vehicles were not allowed. Saturday gave John the opportunity to speak to ophthalmologists and opticians in the morning and patients in the afternoon. A meeting for the medical fraternity was held on Sunday morning after which we enjoyed a delicious lunch on board a yacht sailing around the bay. I even persuaded the captain to let me take a turn at the wheel; nobody saw his guiding hand.

After a promising start with the enthusiastic patient group, it was not possible to establish a Maltese society, but a group continued to inform and help sufferers.

"The coach is fully booked," Beryl Duggan informed me.

"I will have to fly. It won't be a long flight. So I'll go on my own," I responded.

I decided to attend the tenth International Congress of IRPA at Lugano, Switzerland in 1998 having been absent from these meetings for six years. I had been sorry to miss those held in Johannesburg, Paris and Washington where there had been delegates from new member countries. There were thirty-two countries participating in this Congress.

Mary Guest described Lugano as one of the most attractive cities for a Congress. It is set in the Italian-speaking area to the south of Switzerland where everyone seems to switch easily between Italian, French and German. The city surrounds Lake Lugano and much of it is built on the steep hillsides. Each morning we could walk from our hotels to the Congress in the Palazzo di Congressi by the lake.

When I arrived Christina Fasser, who was now the President of IRPA, came forward to greet me. "I have arranged for Tina to guide and help you throughout the Congress," she told me. This was going to be a wonderful help as I could then be independent. She was a confident guide and her command of five languages proved to be invaluable.

"Would you like to meet the two delegates from Japan?" she asked me after the announcement that the Japanese were hoping to host the Congress in four years' time in 2002.

"I think we might have a language problem," I replied.

"There's no problem, I speak Japanese."

It was at this Congress that we changed the name from International Retinitis Pigmentosa Association (IRPA) to Retina International (RI). The change reflected a broader focus on all retinal degenerations which are a major cause of blindness in adult life.

―――◆―――

"Was that the worst flight you've ever had?" I asked Geoff Strutt in the safety and comfort of our Canadian hotel. I knew that he was an experienced air traffic controller with a pilot's licence and had helped to establish the transatlantic air traffic system. It had felt as if we were falling out of the sky as we approached Canada. He and his wife Hilary were accompanying me to the eleventh Congress of Retina International in Toronto.

'VISION QUEST 2000' was an appropriate title given to this Congress held in the Westin Harbour Heights Hotel on the shores of Lake Ontario. The needle-shaped CN Tower dwarfed our skyscraper hotel. Stephen Jones joined me as the other delegate of BRPS in the General Assembly replacing Mary Guest. Eight hundred people attended the Congress, including a large group from the UK. Forty-three countries were represented in all.

Among the thousand attendees at the twelfth Congress in Chiba on Tokyo Bay in 2002, only two of them were British, Stephen Jones, as the BRPS delegate, and Professor Alan Bird. With the emphasis, in the science sessions, on the move towards clinical trials the theme of the Congress was 'EYE ON THE FUTURE'.

Clinical trials were once again the main topic featured at the Dutch Congress in 2004. For the first time the programme included discussion groups for young people. We all appreciated how crucial it was to involve future generations. Hopefully, they would be encouraged by all they heard and inspired to take a more active role in the RP movement.

I had always wanted to visit the house where Anne Frank and her family had hidden from the Gestapo for so long. Also to ride on a tram and visit the diamond factory in Amsterdam. I managed all three on a day of relaxation in the company of my friends Hilary and Geoff Strutt.

The day set aside for 'Workshops' at these international congresses gave us an opportunity to exchange information. It became clear that an idea which was successful in one country would not necessarily work in another. Fundraising was an obvious example.

The Canadians raised large amounts of money every year through their event 'Ride for Sight'. The motorcyclists, known as 'Bikers', were sponsored not only by the general public but also by companies involved in the motorcycle industry. They were sponsored to ride across Canada, as vast as it is.

This was started when a young 'Biker' miserably told his friends that he was losing his sight, due to RP, and he would have to give up the love of his life, his bike. They had the idea of 'Ride for Sight'.

'Sing for Sight' is the French way of raising money each year. All over France choirs, however large or small, participate. On a specified day each choir gives a local concert in aid of RP research.

However hard we tried we could not muster any enthusiasm for these two events in the UK.

All over the world now the third week in September is set aside as 'World Retina Week'. Exchanging Newsletters is another way of keeping information flowing around the world. But it is at meetings of Retina International, when we come together from many different backgrounds, that we are most aware of our common aim to find a way to conquer RP.

Chapter 12

FIGHTING BLINDNESS
Members Help Research

"She would rather light a candle than curse the darkness."
Eleanor Roosevelt 1884-1962

"This young man will certainly further the research effort into RP," John Marshall told the Board of Trustees. In America a young man who had been diagnosed with RP was dying from an incurable form of cancer. He had asked that on his death his eyes should be donated to further the medical research programme into RP.

What a bequest. It became the inspiration for eye donor schemes in America, Canada and the UK. It was one way members could help medical research. Permission had to be obtained from the Department of Health and Social Security in London. Alan Bird and John Marshall carried out all the necessary negotiations. UK Transplants, a service for transporting donor material, agreed to participate in our scheme. BRPS set up six regional areas. A consultant ophthalmologist* in each area was responsible for the removal of donor tissue and preserving it in a suitable form for laboratory use, ready for UK Transplants to arrange transport to the appropriate research laboratory.

Before we could introduce the scheme donor cards had to be designed and produced. Lloyds Bank not only sponsored one thousand donor cards, the size of a normal credit card, they also gave a Press Conference at their head office in London to launch the scheme in June 1980. Our medical research team answered numerous questions from the media. A great deal of interest was aroused.

Within the first few weeks there were five hundred requests for a donor card. Names and addresses were collected at our AGM that month and at the 'See by Touch' exhibition in July. Each person was sent a consent form asking for details of their GP and Ophthalmologist. When the consent form was returned I sent a photocopy of it to the donor's GP and Ophthalmologist. It then went on to a register at the Institute of Ophthalmology*. The donor card must be signed and gives the emergency telephone number for the 24 hour switchboard of the UK Transplant Service, who should be contacted immediately in the event of the donor's death. They then make all further arrangements.

A grant of £6,000 was awarded to Dr John Mellerio (now a Professor) at the Polytechnic of Central London to establish a tissue culture centre. Each donor eye provides only a small number of cells and it was hoped to grow cells in test tubes to supply other laboratories with samples to test and analyse.

By the end of 1980 five pairs of eyes had been received. As a result a much clearer understanding has been developed concerning the ways in which the anatomy of the retina degenerates in the different types of RP. In addition donor eyes have been used for biochemical analysis of the various cells in the retina.

The response we have had to the Eye Donor Scheme shows how much people want to contribute medically to the research programme.

———◆◆———

Over the years members have completed a questionnaire stating their family history and in some cases blood samples were taken.

The world's largest register of RP patients, whose family history can be traced back eight or nine generations, is held at Moorfields Eye Hospital. This is due to the pioneering work, begun in 1979, by Dr Marcelle Jay, wife of Professor Barrie Jay, a Consultant Ophthalmologist at Moorfields. The register is constantly updated by two genetic nurses. It is used to select suitable patients and their families for clinical and molecular genetic research*. Throughout, the project has been funded by BRPS.

Tracing family histories in the Republic of Ireland speeded research work carried out at Trinity College, Dublin.

"There is an urgent telephone message for you," Glynis greeted me as I entered the office late one afternoon in 1989. "Michael Griffith wants you to ring him immediately."

I rang Michael straightaway. As soon as he could be found he came to the telephone. I heard the excitement in his voice.

"The research team, led by Dr Peter Humphries at Trinity College, Dublin, has located the world's first RP gene. It's one that is responsible for Autosomal Dominant RP*," he announced.

"At last!" I thought.

"Can you come over to a Press Conference next week?" Michael asked.

"Just try and keep me away."

BRPS had awarded a grant towards this work.

By the time David and I arrived in Ireland a press release had been sent to the media both in the Irish Republic and the UK. Trinity College was humming with the preparations for this momentous occasion. Michael was being helped by some of the members of the Irish Society to carry the refreshments up the well-worn steps to the conference room. As some of them had RP it was a miracle nothing was broken.

Michael and I joined Peter and his team at the table to answer questions from the many reporters. Television cameras were in place. Peter handled numerous questions about his work, giving a clear description of how RP manifests itself. He explained that locating a gene responsible for it would take us to the next step of correcting that faulty gene.

When the general questions had been answered Peter gave interviews for both television and radio while we mingled with the reporters. The celebrations had only just begun.

In the same year there was more exciting news. A second group of research workers had found a defect in the gene responsible for making rhodopsin*, the light-sensitive pigment inside the eye. This was a different autosomal dominant gene from the one located by Peter Humphries. Within the space of a year groups around the world had identified specific mutations* in the gene responsible for rhodopsin.

This rapidly accelerating pace of discovery led to the location of numerous genes responsible for the different types of RP. By 1996 some laboratories were experimenting in genetic engineering* on retinal tissues by introducing genes in an attempt to correct the genetic deficiencies induced by RP genes. All this work has been dependent upon financial resources funded by BRPS.

Another opportunity for members of the Society to assist

medical research came when we encouraged them to lobby their MPs. Many of us had listened to interviews on the Radio 4 'Today' programme about a Bill which was before Parliament based on a White Paper 'Human Fertilisation and Embryology*'. MPs would have a free vote on two alternative clauses. The first would ban all procedures on a pre-embryo other than those aimed at preparing it for introduction to the womb of a woman undergoing 'In Vitro Fertilisation' (IVF) treatment. The second would permit certain research work to be carried out under licence. This offered hope to sufferers from inherited diseases. I knew a pre-embryo was a minute group of cells which forms during the first fourteen days after fertilisation. If the first clause became law any RP research on pre-embryos would be illegal.

"What should we do?"

On the 8th November 1989 I sat down with the Management Committee to discuss it. We were all aware of the issues of conscience that surround the subject. However, we decided to support the second version. Through the Newsletter we encouraged our members, who agreed with this decision, to write to their MP urging him or her to vote for the clause which would allow research to continue under licence. It never ceases to amaze me how rapidly our members respond to a challenge. We were inundated at the office by copies of their letters sent to MPs and the subsequent replies.

It was early morning on the 7th February 1990 when we embarked on the new experience of lobbying our MPs. Westminster Hall was packed with people, all concerned about research into inherited diseases. The organisers of the Genetic Interest Group (GIG) provided hot soup and rolls for us before Lord Denis Carter took the BRPS group to the Central Lobby in the Houses of Parliament. We each completed and signed a green card giving the name of our MP and the nature of our business. Messengers took away our cards. Time passed. Suddenly, above the hum of conversation I heard my name being called.

Tim Boswell, our MP, soon found me.

By this time the lobby was full of people, representing every type of disability. They were all endeavouring to find their own MP. Many members of both Houses came down to listen to our point of view.

An unexpected item of television news that evening showed me, wet and bedraggled in a raincoat and headscarf, being led by a dripping wet Guide Dog into the Houses of Parliament with Denis Carter.

The day before the Bill was put to the House of Lords, David and I had a further opportunity to discuss it with Members of Parliament over a cup of tea in the Members' Dining Room. We were conspicuous as we wore the Society's bright yellow tabards bearing the words 'Fighting Blindness'. We wanted to make sure that everyone knew why we were there.

The House of Lords voted overwhelmingly in our favour and the Bill became an Act of Parliament later that year.

While the Society was helping to support medical research we were aware that our members had to live each day with the problems of RP. A prominent problem was obtaining the correct protection for our eyes from sunlight.

On my first visit to the Massachusetts Ear and Eye Hospital in 1974 Eliot Berson strongly advised me to wear sunglasses whenever exposed to sunlight all the year round. I was prescribed a pair with top and side shields which blocked light penetrating the eyes from all angles. He was adamant about it because a study had shown that RP patients exposed to sunlight experienced a more rapid deterioration in their eyesight compared to those who had protected their eyes. I thought these glasses were ugly and uncomfortable. I would have to find something better than this I decided.

Some years later when I met Janet Silver at the low vision aid clinic at Moorfields Eye Hospital I faced her with my dilemma.

"I would like a more comfortable and more attractive pair of sunglasses which give me the same protection as these," I declared.

This simple request was to prove far more complex than I had imagined and led to our members participating in a survey of various types of sunglasses.

She explained that ultraviolet light, both UVA and UVB, is toxic and can damage the skin and eyes. Also short-wave length visible light (i.e. blue) causes increased response in the retina compared with similar quantities of long-wave length (i.e. red) light. Hence blue light reaching the eye should be cut to a minimum. In the dark the pupil of the eye dilates, which allows more light to penetrate the retina. Consequently the wrong type of sunglasses may provide the eyes with some darkness, but at the same time allow potentially damaging light to reach the retina. To redress this, the British Standards Institution produced a standard for sunglasses. As well as being good optical quality the lenses must block ultraviolet light (UV).

In the early stages of RP I had realised that a major problem was adaptation to different levels of light. If I entered a room after being out in bright sunlight I could not see anything at all for quite a while. Similarly when I left a well lit room and went out after dark my eyes could take up to half an hour to adapt, whereas a person with normal sight adjusts within two or three minutes. To try and overcome this difficulty I wore glasses with photochromic lenses which darkened depending on the intensity of light.

To my disappointment, I did not find them helpful. Glare was an added complication. Being out in bright sunlight, even with the protection of sunglasses, was particularly painful. To combat glare I tried polarised lenses which can reduce glare considerably. I found these useful for a time. After a great deal of trial and error eventually I settled for glasses with a graduated tint. These had lenses which were quite dark at the top and faded down to more or less clear at the bottom, allowing me good contrast, for example at kerbs. However, all this is an individual choice. What suits one RP patient will not necessarily suit another.

A good example of how patients varied was the red photochromic glass lens produced by the American firm Corning. These lenses cut out most blue light. An experiment was set up when people were given Corning lenses and a matched pair without knowing which was which. Most people preferred the copies, but a few found the Corning lenses had advantages. At least we were pleased our members had the opportunity to participate in the experiment.

We have always been able to rely on our members to respond to any initiative taken by the Society for research.

Chapter 13

EUPHORIA ON THE MOUNTAIN TOPS
Highlights for the Society

"It is a far, far, better thing that I do, than I have ever done."
A Tale of Two Cities. Charles Dickens 1812-1870

Peals of laughter came from my daughter's bedroom. Helen was helping Elaine Harris with her make-up before setting out with me for Westminster Abbey. This was to be the first of many memorable occasions in the history of the Society.

"I don't want to interrupt the fun, but the car will be here soon," I called out.

Elaine, who was blind from birth, appeared at the top of the stairs looking lovely.

This promised to be a momentous day as we travelled to the Abbey with Eric and Hazel Katz in their chauffeur-driven Rolls Royce. I felt sure Yasmin, my Guide Dog, was appreciating this luxurious smooth ride as much as I was.

The splendour of Westminster Abbey was awesome as we took our places for the Thanksgiving and Rededication Service to mark the Centenary of the Ophthalmological Society of the United Kingdom on Wednesday, 16th April 1980.

The Order of Service told us that the object of the Society is the cultivation and promotion of Ophthalmology and it takes an active part in the advancement of the clinical, academic and research aspects of the subject. It also explained that the Thanksgiving Service was being held to inaugurate the Centenary meeting of the Ophthalmological Society and was for all those people who in their several ways serve the art and science devoted to the saving of sight and to helping those denied the gift of sight.

I was seated next to the aisle in the nave of the Abbey so that Yasmin had more space. I could hear Hazel reading the order of service to Eric and Elaine. I struggled to read for myself the names of those in the processions. There were fifteen processions in all, representing the medical fraternity. They all wore academic dress or uniform with the maces and other insignia of the various orders borne before them. This added pageantry to the occasion.

The service was due to start at 11.00am and at 10.35am the first procession entered the Abbey. The Lord Mayor of Westminster was received at the Great West Door by the Dean and Chapter of Westminster at 10.49am and conducted to his seat. His Royal Highness the Duke of Gloucester and his procession were the last to take their seats before the arrival of His Royal Highness, Prince Philip, the Duke of Edinburgh. Everyone in this vast congregation was there by invitation because of their connection with visual impairment.

At the stroke of eleven a fanfare of trumpets sounded. Yasmin jumped to her feet and backed out into the aisle. I pulled her back just in time before the final procession approached. Prince Philip bent down to pat her as he passed.

Well-known hymns and Bible readings referred to the gift of sight or the lack of it either in a physical or spiritual sense. The Right Reverend George Reindorp, Lord Bishop of Salisbury, made a plea to the medical profession in his sermon. He asked all concerned to treat their patients as individuals suffering from a complaint, rather then treating a complaint which happened to take up residence in a person.

I shall always remember the sound of the music which filled the Abbey that day: the fanfare of trumpets played by trumpeters from the Royal Military School of Music, the rich tones of the Abbey organ and the unique voices of the Abbey choir trained to perfection.

The Abbey bells rang out as we left the building, inspired to renew the task of furthering the cause of visual impairment. Bright sunlight enhanced the scene before us. Small groups stood around chatting about the service. The various uniforms of nurses and the military together with the academic robes and robes of the clergy made a colourful picture.

I was opening the mail as usual one morning when my attention was caught by the words, '10 Downing Street, Whitehall'.

"Whatever is this about?" I exclaimed to myself.

Curious, I slit open the envelope.

I read the following: 'The Prime Minister and Mr Denis Thatcher request the honour of the company of Mrs L. Drummond-Walker at a reception for voluntary workers in the health and personal social services field at 10 Downing Street, Whitehall on Monday, 14th July 1980 from 6.30pm to 8.00pm. Uniform optional'.

A colleague of John Marshall offered to drive me to 10 Downing Street with his brother, who also had an invitation. He did not tell me that it was a two seater open top sports car. Yasmin and I climbed into the back. I was relieved it was only a short drive from Victoria station to Downing Street.

It was an experience to go through the famous door which is featured so often in the media. Yasmin led me across the black and white checked floor of the entrance hall to the lift. Arriving at the reception I was introduced to Mrs Thatcher. Her interest in the cause and symptoms of RP, ways in which the eye donor scheme could further medical research and her concern for me revealed a gentleness I had not associated with her as the 'iron lady'. It was not long before Denis Thatcher came up to me, intrigued by Yasmin, who was sitting patiently by my side with one eye on the food. He wanted to know how Guide Dogs are trained and the difference she made to my life. Mrs Thatcher reappeared bearing a plate of canapés. "May I give your dog some of these?" she enquired.

"Certainly not. Guide Dogs are kept to a strict diet."

"What a pity."

Laughing I replied, "Now I can tell people that the Prime Minister has obeyed me!"

I then expressed a wish to see the Cabinet Room. Kindly she took me to the door of the Cabinet Room and I was allowed to have a peep inside.

After meeting some members of the Cabinet and mingling with fellow guests I requested a taxi. As I sank into the taxi seat I thought back over the events of the evening. Never in my wildest dreams did I think I would go to a Reception at 10 Downing Street and converse with so many famous politicians.

We arrived at the Governors Hall, St Thomas' Hospital on 17th March 1992 to find that security was high. John Marshall would be giving his inaugural lecture in the presence of HRH the Duchess of Gloucester. I was thrilled that John had been appointed Frost Professor of Ophthalmology at St Thomas' Hospital. His lecture was entitled 'Lasers and the Eye – Photon Surgery*'. I have heard John speak many times and on this occasion he was truly inspirational. Among his various gifts he is a great orator.

His family and friends in the audience were very proud of him.

I thought back to the day, seventeen years earlier, when I first met John. Little did I know then all that he was to achieve.

His research over the past thirty years has ranged over a number of ocular problems. He has concentrated on the inter-relationships between light and ageing as well as the mechanisms underlying age-related, diabetic and inherited retinal disease. He has been involved in the development of lasers for use in ophthalmic surgery and patented the revolutionary Excimer laser for the correction of refractive disorders. He also created the world's first Diode laser for treating the eye problems of diabetes, glaucoma and ageing.

John has been awarded more than twenty honours worldwide and is an Honorary Fellow of both The Royal College of Ophthalmologists and Cardiff University. He has sat on and chaired many national and international committees and acted as a scientific advisor to several grant-giving charities in addition to our own.

How fortunate we are to have had the support of someone so able and exceptional – support which continues to this day.

The evening of his inaugural lecture concluded with a champagne reception. Two hundred guests crowded into the room, all involved with work related to visual science. There were medical research scientists, ophthalmologists and representatives of various charities for the blind, who sponsored medical research. Trays of champagne and orange juice were served. Suddenly I heard a glass being knocked over and my Guide Dog, Snowy, licking the floor. Unfortunately the orange juice had soaked his head as well. By the time I was introduced to the Chairman of the GDBA Snowy's curls were a sticky mess and standing on end.

This was a double celebration for us because Shomi Bhattacharya succeeded John as Sembal Professor of

Experimental Ophthalmology at the Institute of Ophthalmology. He would head the new department of Molecular Genetics* there.

In the autumn of the same year we had a grand royal week. On Wednesday, 14th October David and I drove to London for the opening ceremony of the new Ashton Building. This was part of the relocated Institute of Ophthalmology* adjacent to Moorfields Eye Hospital. David left me at the entrance while he parked the car. Professor Norman Ashton, one of the world's most eminent ocular pathologists*, was one of our medical advisors. It was a great tribute to his work that the new building was named after him.

We all waited for HRH the Prince Andrew to arrive following his conducted tour of the new laboratories. David went to check the car.

"I think we are parked beside the Prince's car," he said on his return. "There is a private detective guarding the car."

After the unveiling of the plaque by the Prince we had an interesting tour ourselves.

We were back in London the next day at Broadcasting House. This time we were attending the 'David Scott Blackhall Memorial Award' presented by HRH the Princess Royal for the 'In Touch' programme. David Scott Blackhall had been the programme's presenter for the first twenty years of its existence. He had a revolutionary approach to blindness, dealing with it in a matter of fact and amusing way. Judy Sarssam, a member of BRPS, had nominated Pat Crane for her invention of the Eezee Reader* scanning device. After the presentation David again went to check the car and to his surprise he found the same private detective as the day before guarding the royal car.

The following Monday I had tea with HRH the Princess Alexandra at the GDBA training centre in Leamington Spa. There was no royal detective next to our car this time for the Princess left by helicopter.

"Happy Birthday. I've brought your mail. There are a lot of cards and a letter from 10 Downing Street," called a voice from downstairs. Caroline, my hairdresser, was washing my hair ready for a family birthday party that evening.

The letter lay unopened among my birthday cards until my secretary returned to join us for a cup of coffee. Above the noise of the hairdryer I heard her exclaim, "Goodness gracious me. You are being awarded an MBE in the New Year Honours List." The hairdryer stopped. The letter was read to me. I could not believe it. It was only after the letter had been read to me again that it began to register. Enclosed with the letter was a form of acceptance for me to complete and send back by return of post. I was asked not to tell anyone, except my immediate family, until after 12 noon on the day before the list was published. That was the difficult part.

A beautiful bouquet of flowers arrived on the 31st December 1993 from Jenny and Alan Rudge. This was the first of many messages of congratulations. The telephone rang constantly. Word soon spread. I was overwhelmed by the excitement of friends and members of the Society.

I was informed by the Central Chancery of the Orders of Knighthood, St James's Palace, that the Investiture would be held at Buckingham Palace on Thursday 17th February 1994. I was allowed to take three guests and NO MORE and must arrive between 10.00am and 10.30am.

As I had no sight at all by this time I needed help to choose my outfit. Helen, my daughter, and my American friend, Susan Freeland, offered to come on a shopping spree in London. We arrived home triumphantly, after a happy and exhausting day, having purchased our outfits for the occasion.

The clock struck 5.00am as we crept downstairs for a hot drink before leaving for London an hour later on the day of the Investiture. David had planned the day to the last detail. Helen, Anthony, David and I had a splendid breakfast at the Royal Automobile Club in Pall Mall where we were able to change into our smart clothes. The doorman of the club was a little surprised, as we left, to see David and Anthony in morning dress with their top hats accompanying mother and daughter who were also wearing large hats.

We drove the short distance to Buckingham Palace, entering at the Main Gate. There were police everywhere. Two stepped forward to check the car thoroughly: inside, outside, underneath and in the boot where our suitcases were opened. When they were satisfied they waved us on. As we had a car sticker indicating a disability we were allowed to go under the arch into the inner courtyard.

Ray, one of the Queen's pages, was waiting to receive us. He took us upstairs in a lift while the other recipients walked up the Grand Staircase. My family was shown into the Ballroom where the Investiture would take place. Ray guided me to the Picture Gallery to be briefed about the ceremony. A small hook was attached to the left-hand side of my jacket so that the medal could be hung without any difficulty. We were informed that the Queen usually gave every recipient their medal but, as she had her arm in a sling after a riding accident, her Lord Chamberlain would be performing that part of the Ceremony on behalf of Her Majesty. After a few trial curtsies I was really nervous in spite of

Ray's reassurance that he would be beside me throughout.

The briefing continued with a detailed description of what would happen in the Ballroom. Two hundred gilt chairs were set out in rows immediately in front of the dais, on which stood the two thrones under a silk canopy. Most of our guests would sit on tiered banquettes around the walls. The Queen would enter the Ballroom as the Band of the Welsh Guards played 'Men of Harlech', their regimental march. They would play softly in the background throughout the ceremony. The Queen would be accompanied by the Lord Chamberlain and two Gurkha Orderly officers. Five members of the Yeomen of the Guard, the oldest military bodyguard in the world, would already be in position behind the thrones. Behind the Queen would follow The Controller of the Lord Chamberlain's office, with several members of the staff.

When we approached the entrance to the State Ballroom Ray whispered that we were joining the line of recipients waiting to be announced. We could hear the Chief Usher calling the names. We moved forward as each name was called in alphabetical order.

After Shirley Bassey's name was called the Welsh Guards struck up the theme tune of the song she sang for the James Bond film 'Goldfinger'. On this occasion she received her first award, the OBE.

A few more names were called.

"Lynda Mary Cantor."

An encouraging nudge from Ray and we walked into the Ballroom. He had carefully explained that he would indicate by squeezing my arm, that I was directly in front of the Queen. It was at this point that I had to turn, curtsey and walk five steps forward. The medal was presented to me and Her Majesty formally congratulated me. I took five steps back, but in my nervousness forgot to curtsey again. Ray guided me to an anteroom where I was struck by the pungent smell of leather. My medal was placed in a leather box before we returned to the Ballroom. We sat on one of the gilt chairs to enjoy the rest of the Ceremony. At the conclusion of the Ceremony the Welsh Guards played the National Anthem and the Queen led her Household out of the Ballroom.

I rejoined my family to walk down the Grand Staircase instead of taking the lift. There was a guard of honour from the Household Cavalry on alternate stairs. It was a bitterly cold day so we did not linger long for our photographs to be taken outside the Palace.

We were pleased to return to the warmth of the Royal Automobile Club for a celebratory lunch. We were joined by my Aunt Jessie, John and Judith Marshall, also John and Tessa Grindle. A perfect end to a momentous occasion. I felt I had received this decoration on behalf of all our members, who had worked so hard and achieved so much.

By 1997 we had amongst our members many who had shown considerable fortitude in overcoming their visual problem to raise funds for the Society through sponsorship of their sporting events. We decided to recognise their achievements by inviting them to a presentation evening on the 17th June in the restaurant at the top of the Telecom Tower in London. This was kindly arranged once again by our Chairman Alan Rudge.

We thought it would be appropriate if the Minister for Sport in the new Labour Government, Mr Tony Banks, would present a trophy to mark each individual achievement. Unbeknown to Colin and Linda McArthur, who had organised the evening, Sir Campbell Adamson, our President, and Tony Banks were old friends. Together they made it a lively and remarkable occasion.

The members who were honoured for their achievements included:

Steve Bateman who has completed several marathons and long distance tandem cycle runs, plus a parachute jump.

Jim Bithell, who organised national championships for visually impaired bowlers around the country, which involves the scheduling of around 400 matches per championship.

Phil Gibson, a marathon runner who has run the London Marathon and has organised the St Albans half marathon.

Roger Green, Chairman of our Management Committee, completed the Land's End to John o'Groats tandem ride in 8 days and also competed in the Tulip Marathon.

Ben Jones, our youngest achiever who, at 17 years of age, climbed above the 19,000ft mark on Mount Kilimanjaro in an expedition organised by World Challenge.

Philip Jones, who has run the London Marathon and also did a parachute jump.

Graham Lowe, who has taken part in the London Marathon several times.

Marion Mansfield, who was a rider in the 'Eye to Sea' tandem ride.

Kate Newitt, who won a gold medal in the first International Blind Sailing Regatta in New Zealand.

Nicola Newman, who organised many fundraising sporting events whilst at school, including an 8 mile fun run.

Dr Mike Newton, who completed the 192 mile coast to coast walk which, with its many ups and downs, involved a total of 24,000ft of climbing.

Linda Wesley, an all-rounder involved in tandem rides, sailing, gliding and bowls.

Dave Winsper, who has completed the London Marathon and was the first blind person to complete the 50 miles Long Mynd

Hike in 23 hours. He has completed the Land's End to John o'Groats tandem ride twice.

It was a very special evening to acknowledge the courage and sheer determination of these members.

"This is one of Elizabeth Frink's sculptures commissioned by the Development Corporation for this new town," my Guide Dog trainer explained to me. We were standing in front of a large bronze statue in the shopping centre of Milton Keynes. Little did I know at the time, that in 1997 I would be chosen by a Panel of Judges as one of the finalists for the Elizabeth Frink Award.

The Frink Award was founded in 1986 by 'The Women of the Year Lunch' to celebrate the outstanding achievements of visually impaired women. It was so named because the First Prize each year is a beautiful winged eagle bronze statuette donated to 'The Women of the Year Lunch' by Dame Elizabeth Frink. In addition to holding the sculpture for one year the winner receives a commemorative medallion of the Award and a cheque for £1,000. 'The Women of the Year Lunch' is a charity which in the past raised money for the Greater London Fund for the Blind.

As the winner of third prize in 1997 I was invited to the Press Launch in the Boardroom at Moorfields Eye Hospital on Wednesday 17th September and to 'The Women of the Year Lunch' at the Savoy Hotel, London on Monday 6th October.

When we arrived at the Savoy Hotel the lobby was very busy. There were women everywhere and it was both a relief and a pleasure to meet my old friend Janet Silver. She suggested we find our table early and as we entered the dining room I was struck by the scent of orchids. Janet described the arrangements of orchids on each table. These had been donated by a large company in memory of Diana, Princess of Wales.

The sound of conversation filled the room as women who had been exceptionally successful in their chosen vocation exchanged experiences over lunch. After lunch Floella Benjamin, the chairman, introduced the Royal Guest of Honour, Her Majesty Queen Noor of Jordan, who presented the Awards. The first prize was won by Mrs Elaine Noad, the Director of Community Services for South Ayrshire Council. The second prize was won by twenty-five year old Louise Ann Byles, the first blind person to qualify as a Clinical Psychologist in Britain.

After the Awards were presented Elaine Noad gave such a vivid account of her work that it was easy to empathise with all she was attempting to do. Queen Noor spoke about her work to improve human welfare in the Middle East. The other speakers were the Right Honourable Harriet Harman MP, Secretary of State for Social Security and Minister for Women and Vivienne Westwood, a British fashion designer. All the talks contributed to the theme of the lunch that year, 'Women Making a Difference'.

By the time I was invited as a guest to 'The Women of the Year Lunch' in 2003 the format had changed. There were now three different Awards. The Good Housekeeping Outstanding Achievement Award which acknowledges an outstanding achievement where courage and determination are often the only spurs to keep going.

The Pilkington 'Window to the World' Award which salutes a woman whose work and courage, in often dangerous or intimidating circumstances, has opened our eyes to a world we would otherwise not have understood.

The Frink Award which recognises two great strengths in women. First, it acknowledges that the recipient has made a difference to the lives of others. Second, this Award recognises an achievement in overcoming what would be, for most of us, unbelievable odds.

"May I have another ticket for the BRPS Publicity Manager, Mireille Portlock?" I asked the organiser of the lunch in 2003. I had asked Mireille if she would accompany me and write an account of the day for our Newsletter.

As we mingled among the guests before sitting down to lunch Mireille whispered that she could see the Calendar Girls. I was more interested to meet Denise Leigh, who had been chosen recently from three thousand hopefuls in a television talent hunt. The programme 'Operatunity' on Channel 4 had set out to find an amateur singer to take the lead role in an English National Opera production of Verdi's 'Rigoletto'. Denise, who has RP, had to count her steps across the stage to avoid falling into the orchestra pit during the performance.

We made our way across the room, "Congratulations, Denise, on your wonderful achievement," I said.

Susan Townsend, the popular authoress, who wrote 'The Diaries of Adrian Mole' among other books, was the winner of the Frink Award that year. She has shown great courage since she was diagnosed with diabetes leading to a rapid loss of her eyesight.

The criteria for the Frink Award could apply to the achievements of many of our members.

―――◆―――

Later in the year after I had finished going through the mail with Kate in the office she said,

"Lynda, you have been short-listed for the Beacon Prize."

"What is that?" I asked.

"The Beacon Fellowship is a new Charitable Trust supported by five founder partners: Charities Aid Foundation (CAF), The Giving Campaign, Classic FM, The Daily Telegraph and Bell Pottinger in addition to a corporate sponsor, Regus," she explained. "It awards six annual prizes to individuals who have made exceptional contributions either to charitable causes or to organisations that benefit the public. The overall winner will be given a cash award of £20,000 for a charity of their choice."

Although I was not given a cash prize I was Highly Commended which meant I was automatically entered for the following year 2004 when again I was Highly Commended. This time the category of Leadership, for which I was entered, was won by Bob Geldof.

Another ongoing occasion commenced on 10th December 2001. An appropriate tribute to my late aunt, Dr Jessie Mole, in recognition of her outstanding contribution to BRPS, was an annual lectureship established in her name. It was to be given each year at the Oxford Symposium of Ophthalmology.

Every year a commemorative silver round medal is struck. Stamped on one side is the following:

BRITISH RETINITIS PIGMENTOSA SOCIETY

Fighting Blindness

DR JESSIE MOLE MEMORIAL MEDAL
1916 – 2000

The other side is engraved with the name of the person giving the lecture and the year.

The inaugural lecture was given by Professor Alan Bird on the subject 'The Prospects of Treatment of Inherited Retinal Diseases'. Sitting in the lecture hall listening to Alan I wished my aunt could have been with us. Jessie had lived the majority of her life in the Oxford area and enjoyed the atmosphere and stimulus of the University City. Oxford, together with the work to conquer RP and her Christian faith were of the utmost importance to her until the end of her life. No tribute could be more fitting for her.

My thoughts went back to the day she and I had sat together beneath her apple tree discussing the possibility of starting a charity. My dream had been to raise enough money to fund all the research needed to find a cure for RP. At the time it was only a dream. A dream we had shared.

Alan continued his lecture.

The dream was beginning to take shape.

On all these special occasions I felt I was representing the members of BRPS. This was a privilege. One which gave me great joy. RP has stolen my eyesight but it has also given me many treasured memories.

EPILOGUE

*"God grant me the serenity to accept the things I cannot change,
the courage to change the things I can
and the wisdom to know the difference."*
Reinhold Niebuhr 1892-1971

Treatment trials for patients with RP are inevitable. Everyone is talking about them. But when will they be available for us all? I would like to know the end of this story as much as anyone. One thing is certain. Future generations will benefit from the dedication and work of numerous people since 1975. A work which continues whether it is the Helpline, Medical Research, Administration, Fundraising or contact one with the other.

What of the future?
We have one centre for genotyping RP patients in Manchester led by Professor Graeme Black already. Will there be others?
Will we see a national centre totally devoted to medical research into retinal degeneration?
Will we see area centres for administering treatments?

This is an unfinished story ... the ending of which will be told by others.

APPENDIX 1

A Report on the Medical Research Progress to date by Selwyn Higgins

*"And many strokes though with a little axe,
Hew down and fell the hardest timbered oak."*
King Henry VI Part III. William Shakespeare 1564-1616

The origins of Retinitis Pigmentosa (RP) are not known but it is possible that the many recorded incidents of people throughout history with slowly deteriorating sight were actually describing people suffering from RP. The disease was first given a name by a Dr Donders in the mid nineteenth century and he chose the name Retinitis Pigmentosa due to the visible pigmentation on the retina. Today we would probably describe the condition as retinal dystrophy*.

The retina is the light-sensitive film in the back of the eye and can be likened to the film in a camera. In a camera, light enters through a diaphragm; it passes through a lens where it is focused onto the film in the back of the camera. This film can be developed to produce a picture. The process in an eye is very similar. The lens in the front of the eye focuses light onto the retina, which is a multi-layer film containing millions of light-sensitive cells called photoreceptor cells. These respond according to the intensity of light seen by each one and relay this information, via the optic nerve, to the brain, where it is processed into a picture. There are two types of photoreceptor cells, called rods and cones, and these will be described in more detail later in this section.

There was very little research into Retinitis Pigmentosa until the mid 1970s. There had been isolated examples of interested scientists carrying out limited investigations but these were mainly concerned with either establishing characteristics of the family with the disease or the nature and structure of changes in the retina. Anyone diagnosed with RP was simply told that they had a rare eye condition that would lead eventually to blindness and that there was no cure. Some were told the name of the condition. It has been explained in this book how this led to the foundation of BRPS, to bring together people with RP to provide mutual support and work towards a cure. Similar organisations were in existence in the USA and Finland.

Although the BRPS was founded in 1975, it was not possible to finance any research projects until a research fund had been built up to a viable level by 1978. The early work involved the development of equipment that would accurately measure deterioration in the retinas of patients, in order to document disease progression in the retina.

It had been recognised for many years that the condition was inherited and like so many inherited conditions it followed three common paths. These are autosomal dominant*, where the disease is passed on by one or both parents of either sex through the dominant gene; autosomal recessive*, where parents who are both unwitting carriers may pass on the condition through a recessive gene* and thirdly X-linked*, where the disease follows a more complex inheritance pattern. In X-linked RP, the disease affects only males and passes from a man to his grandson, via a daughter carrier. Full details of these patterns are given in the BRPS booklet 'Genetics and RP'.

It became obvious at an early stage that any chance of finding a cure lay in finding the genes responsible for RP. A gene is, in effect, a set of instructions for producing a particular protein within the body. The search began in earnest and in 1984, two scientists, Dr Alan Wright and Dr Shomi Bhattacharya, working in Newcastle-on-Tyne University, discovered a marker* that indicated the position of an RP gene. It was becoming apparent that there might be more than one gene and in 1989 Dr Peter Humphries, working in Trinity College, Dublin, was first to identify an RP gene. The following year, two more were found and it soon became clear that there would be many others, explaining why there appeared to be so many variations in RP between patients. It was clear that RP was not a single disease, but a group of diseases, all with similar symptoms and caused by faults in different genes.

As stated above, a gene is a set of instructions. These instructions are responsible for providing the 'blueprint' for all of the characteristics of our body. Each of the cells in our blood, muscle tissues, nerves etc contains twenty-three pairs of chromosomes, one pair inherited from each parent. These chromosomes are long strings of DNA which take the form of a double helix. Picture a very long ladder, then take hold of each end and twist. This perhaps best describes the form of this double helix. We are interested in the cross links, which would be the rungs in the twisted ladder described above. These cross links or bases consist of pairs of chemicals of which there are four kinds represented by the symbols A,C,G and T in a complex pattern of permutations. Groups of these base pairs, in a chain, are known as a gene.

The process of finding an RP gene is very time-consuming. For example the search could cover a chromosomal region of more than 30 million of these base pairs. Scientists have found over 100 gene faults linked to RP over the past 15 years and work on some of the earlier discoveries has now reached an advanced stage. The work can be categorised into three stages, although these can in turn be subdivided. First, find the gene. Second, assess its function and its related biochemistry. Third, develop appropriate corrective genetic and/or non-genetic treatments.

In parallel to this work of finding faulty genes, successful means of introducing the corrective genetic material into an eye have been developed. Minute organisms called viruses are adept at entering cells. Techniques have been developed which utilise this ability and involve taking a virus, removing its disease-carrying genes and adding the corrective genetic material. This viral vector* is then injected into an eye and enters the required cells. Using an adeno-associated* virus vector*, this technique has been used repeatedly, with proven success, in animals which happen to be natural sufferers of RP.

I mentioned above the three principal stages in the research plan. Work on the second stage is wide-ranging as it is now known that the genetic faults causing RP can express themselves in many areas of the retina in order to cause a range of diseases but with symptoms that are outwardly similar. They can, for example, affect the structure of the rod cells*; the ability of photoreceptor cells* to transmit electrical signals; the light responding chemical within the rod cells known as rhodopsin* and affect the pigment epithelium which is crucial in photoreceptor cell survival and function.

Genes (sets of instructions) are responsible for producing a wide range of proteins, which are all required for the structure and functioning of these cells. Following the discovery and analysis of many genes, the array of knowledge accumulated in fifteen years, regarding the biochemistry surrounding RP genes, is now vast. To take just one example, it was discovered around 1990 that, in the long chain molecule forming rhodopsin, a gene fault causes a change in one of the chemicals in the chain. At one point in the chain is a chemical called proline, which responds by changing shape when light falls upon it. This could be an important clue as to how rhodopsin transforms light into an electrical charge. However, if the instruction to produce rhodopsin has been received from an inherited RP gene, the chemical proline is replaced by histidine, which does not react to light. In another type of RP, a gene has been found to be responsible for the faulty production of a chemical called phosphodiesterase, which plays a critical part in allowing photoreceptor cells to build up and discharge electrical charges, which are transmitted to the brain. These two examples form just a tiny part of the knowledge pool now available on the chemistry related to RP genes and it explains why the scientists tell us that RP is a large family of closely related diseases.

Several possible routes for treatment are currently under investigation. These can be grouped as: 1) Gene therapy, 2) Pharmaceutical methods, 3) Stem cell therapy, 4) Tissue transplants and Artificial implants. Let us take a look first at gene therapy.

Gene therapy is based upon the principle of replacing faulty inherited genes with genes that are healthy which, in turn, will transmit accurate information for the production of the necessary proteins. The techniques differ based upon the method by which the RP was inherited. In the case of recessively inherited RP, two faulty genes, one from each parent, fail to perform the function correctly. The technique here is to introduce a healthy functioning gene that will simply take over the function of the faulty RP gene. In the case of RP that is inherited by the dominant route, i.e. the inherited gene is not just faulty but dominant, the process is more complicated. In addition to introducing the healthy gene, it is also necessary to disable the dominant faulty gene, otherwise this would keep overriding the instructions from the correct gene. The instructions from the gene are carried by a substance known as messenger RNA* and it has been shown possible to use small pieces of RNA called ribozymes* to interrupt the RNA that is carrying the faulty instructions, allowing through the instructions from the newly introduced gene.

Pharmaceutical methods involve the introduction into the eye of certain products designed to preserve the cells of the retina. Perhaps a good example of this is the use of ciliary neurotropic factor (CNTF). This is a substance which falls into the group described as survival factors, which have been shown to protect retinal cells against degeneration. Unfortunately, it does not last a long time after injection into the eye. It is not practical to continually inject such a substance into the eye but in 2003, a group in the USA began a phase 1 human trial where tiny slow release spheres containing CNTF are introduced into the eye.

Recently, scientists working in France have discovered clues that could explain why cone cells* cease working after the loss of the last rod cells*. The answer appears to be a protein secreted by the rod cells, which is necessary to support cone cell function. In other words, the cone cells are dependent upon their neighbouring rod cells in order to work and when a significant number of rod cells die, the cone cells begin to shut down. This leads to the question, can we reproduce what the rod cells provide. Scientists have named the protein secreted by the rod cells 'rod derived cone viability factor' (RdCVF) and research carried out in laboratory dishes has shown that chicken cone cells can be made to survive longer by adding a survival factor from mouse rod cells. If this can be artificially produced and introduced into eyes either by a gene therapy approach or periodically administered using a slow release technique, it may be possible to preserve central vision after the loss of the last rod cell.

Stem cell therapy could be the ultimate answer but it is still in its infancy at the time of writing. Stem cells are cells that exist in all parts of the body but which do not have any recognised function. They appear to be waiting to be given a job to do. Different stem cells exist at various points in the body's lifespan. There are embryonic stem cells*, foetal stem cells* and adult stem cells*. Stem cells have been found in the eye of an eighty year old. Stem cells have the ability to multiply, producing more stem cells. Using this ability, they can be 'trained' to grow into photoreceptor cells* or other retinal cells. They are described in detail in the BRPS booklet 'Stem Cell Therapy'.

It may be possible that stem cells could be grown into workable photoreceptor cells in the laboratory and transplanted into an eye, to replace dead cells. There are, however, many problems to be overcome before this can be attempted. There are the usual problems of possible rejection and making contact with appropriate nerve cells but there is a further problem that must be overcome. When it is possible to make stem cells divide/differentiate into appropriate cells that will continue to grow in the retina, it will be necessary to find a way to stop the process at a required point, or face the prospect of uncontrolled growth.

The use of tissue transplants involves replacing a small section of retina with a healthy sample that will, it is hoped, grow into the damaged retina forming a healthy area that will respond to light and send co-ordinated signals back to the brain. Work in this field is progressing with encouraging results but many hurdles need still to be overcome.

The term 'artificial implants' refers to the implantation of man-made devices into the eye in such a way that its natural function may be replicated. A widely explored approach uses tiny photodiode arrays that generate small electrical signals when stimulated by light, in the same way that a photoreceptor cell does. These have faced many problems such as damage to the host retina and rejection. However, the principal problem remains that of connecting the signals from these man-made devices to the system of nerves that connect to the optic nerve, in such a way that the signals arrive at the brain in a manner that will enable a coherent picture to be produced. Refinement in manufacture now means that they can be produced with a cell diameter only ten times greater than that of a natural cell. If this method can be perfected, it may open the way to restoration of sight in an eye that has lost its photoreceptor cells, provided the fine network of nerve cells that connect to the optic nerve are still in working order.

The paragraphs above have outlined the five routes currently under investigation as possible means of halting sight loss due to Retinitis Pigmentosa and possibly improving vision. Others undoubtedly will arise as progress in research continues but on the basis of present results, proof of principle has been established in several areas and it appears that gene therapy (and the use of survival factors) are both methods showing a high possibility of eventual success. In some areas the work is now entering the period of viability trials and these can be extensive and costly but it is a stage that must be passed in order to arrive at safe and workable treatments for Retinitis Pigmentosa.

APPENDIX 2

The Medical and Scientific Advisory Board for the BRPS

Prof John Marshall BSc PhD
(Chairman of BRPS Medical Advisors)
St Thomas' Hospital
London

Prof R Ali BSc PhD
Institute of Ophthalmology

Prof DB Archer FRCS FRCOphth
Royal Victoria Hospital
Belfast

Prof G B Arden BSc MB BS PhD
London

Dr K C Barnett OBE MA PhD BSc DVOphthal FRCVS Dip ECVO
Animal Health Trust
Newmarket

Prof S Bhattacharya BSc PhD
Institute of Ophthalmology
London

Prof A C Bird MD FRCS FRCOphth
Moorfields Eye Hospital
London

Prof M E Boulton BSc PhD
Cardiff University

Dr C Converse ScB PhD
Department of Pharmaceutical Sciences
University of Strathclyde

Prof A Dick BSc MD FRCP FRCS FRCOphth
Bristol Eye Hospital

Prof A Fielder FRCP FRCS FRCOphth
Western Eye Hospital
London

Prof F Fitzke BA PhD
Institute of Ophthalmology
London

Prof J V Forrester MD FRCSE FRCOphth FRCSG
Department of Ophthalmology
University of Aberdeen

Dr J Gill BSc MSc PhD CEng MIEE RNIB
Great Portland Street
London

Prof S A Hodson BSc PhD
University of Wales
Cardiff

Prof B Jay BSc PhD
London

Dr M Jay BSc PhD
London

Prof J Mellerio BSc PhD
Westminster University
London

Prof A T Moore MA FRCS FRCOphth
Institute of Ophthalmology
Moorfields Eye Hospital
London

Prof M J Neal BSc MA PhD DSc
St Thomas' Hospital
London

Mr E S Rosen MD FRCS FRCOphth
Visiting Professor
Dept of Vision Science UMIST
Manchester

Miss Janet Silver OBE MPhil FBOA FBIM FAOO
London

Prof A F Wright MB ChB PhD MRC Psych
Western General Hospital
Edinburgh

GLOSSARY

A

Adeno-associated virus	A virus often found in cells simultaneously infected with Adenovirus. However, by itself it seems to be harmless. In the context of the text a special virus whose own genetic material has been removed and replaced by a normal gene to combat an RP gene.
Adult stem cells	Undifferentiated cells found amongst mature cells in a tissue or organ. They can differentiate into the major specialised cells in that organ.
Amniotic membrane	A membrane like the innermost layer of the placenta that supports embryonic cells.
Autosomes	All chromosomes excluding the sex chromosomes.
Autosomal dominant RP	RP is known to exist in a family. It can affect both males and females. There is a 50% chance of an affected parent passing it to a child.
Autosomal recessive RP	Both parents carry the faulty gene and have a 25% chance of having a child with the condition. There is usually no known history of RP in the family.

C

Cataract	A clouding in the lens of the eye.
Central vision	The main line of sight.
Choroideremia	The choroid which lies beneath the retina slowly degenerates. This damages the rods and eventually the cones of the retina. The mode of inheritance is X-linked, i.e. the females within a family are the carriers.

	They have 50% chance of passing it to their sons.
Chromosomes	The cells of our body contain 23 pairs of chromosomes consisting of DNA made up of genes.
Cloned gene	Finding out the exact nature of a gene in order to identify the chemical change causing an inherited disease.
Cone cells	A few million cells called cones are concentrated in the central portion of the retina. They enable us to see fine detail and colour.
Crystallography	The science of crystal form and structure.

E

Eezee Reader scanning device	A hand held scanner connected to a box into which the TV aerial is plugged. The scanner is run over the material to be read which appears enlarged on the television screen.
Embryo	An unborn baby in the first eight weeks from conception.
Embryology	A study of embryos,
Embryonic stem cells	Stem cells from embryos derived from in vitro fertilisation. They can differentiate into any cell type.

F

Foetal stem cells	Stem cells derived from foetuses.

G

Gene	An inherited unit composed of DNA that determines particular characteristics of an individual.

Gene mapping for RP	Finding the chromosome on which genes causing RP are situated.
Gene therapy	Introduction of genetic material into cells for therapeutic purposes.
Genetic engineering	The manipulation of DNA for the transformation of genes in order to modify the characteristics of an organism.
Genetic eye clinic	An eye clinic dealing with inherited diseases.
Genetic inheritance	Characteristics inherited from parents by the genes.
Genetic material	Consists of genes.
Genome	The map of human genes.
Genotyping	Investigating the genetic constitution of an individual.
Gyrate atrophy	An autosomal recessive type of RP which usually presents between 10-40 years of age, characterised by progressive night blindness and peripheral vision loss.

I

Identified gene	Identifying the chemical change in a gene causing an inherited disease.
Institute of Ophthalmology	A research centre attached to Moorfields Eye Hospital.
Isolated gene	A gene with the desired characteristics for which the sequence of the genome is available for use in a laboratory.

L

Laurence-Moon-Bardet-Biedl Syndrome (LMBBS)	A rare, recessive, inherited disorder. The characteristics include visual impairment caused by rod-cone dystrophy, sometimes diagnosed as RP.

Located gene	A gene for which the exact position in the genome has been established.

M

Marker	A small region of DNA along a chromosome that can be used to indicate the location of a gene or other DNA sequence.
Messenger	RNA Genetic material that encodes and carries information from DNA to sites where a protein is made.
Modes of inheritance for RP	Various ways of inheriting different types of RP: autosomal dominant, recessive or X-linked.
Molecular genetics	Concerned with the structure and nature of genes at the level of DNA.
Mutations in genes	A change in the chemical make up of a gene.

O

Ocular pathologist	A pathologist specialising in the study of diseases of the eye.
Ophthalmology	The scientific study of the eye.
Ophthalmologist	An eye specialist.
Ophthalmic departments	Hospital departments concerned with the treatment of eyes.
Ophthalmic optician	A specialist who deals with examining eyes for the purpose of prescribing glasses/contact lenses.
Orthoptic clinic	A clinic concerned with squints and eye movement disorders (rather like physiotherapy for the eye).
Oxford Congress of Ophthalmology	An annual congress of ophthalmologists meeting in Oxford.

P

Peripheral vision	The ability to see outside the main line of sight i.e. to the sides, above and below.
Photon surgery	Cutting tissue using highly focused light beam.
Photoreceptor cells	Millions of cells within the retina which respond to light.
Pigmentation of the retina	In the normal eye pigment is found in a single layer behind the retina called the pigment epithelium. In an RP eye those cells may migrate forward into the retina.

R

Recessive mode of inheritance	Both parents carry the same faulty gene and pass it onto their child who develops the disease. The parents will probably not have the disease themselves.
Research Fellowship	A scientist within a laboratory who may be funded by various charitable organisations/grants.
Retina	Light-sensitive tissue which lines the inside of the eye at the back.
Retinal atrophy/degeneration	Disease in which the retina degenerates or loses its structure and function due to inherited or acquired causes.
Retinal diagnostic clinic	A hospital clinic which diagnoses diseases of the retina.
Retinal dystrophy	A form of inherited retinal degeneration due to a gene defect.
Rhodopsin	The light-sensitive pigment in rod cells.
Ribozymes	Small pieces of RNA that can speed up a chemical reaction.
Rod cells	Rod cells are positioned away from the central portion of the retina. They enable us to see when light is dim and provide peripheral vision outside of the main line of sight.

S
Sequenced gene	Gene whose code has been determined.

U
Usher Syndrome	Impaired hearing and sight. A recessive mode of inheritance. Both parents are carriers of the same Usher gene and have passed it on to their child. The parents will probably not have Usher themselves.
Type 1	Born profoundly deaf. Develop RP in childhood or adolescence.
Type 2	Born partially hearing. Develop RP in adolescence.
Type 3	Born with normal hearing and sight. Develop hearing impairment and RP in adolescence or later in life.

V
Viral vector	A virus that has been genetically engineered to deliver a specific molecule(s) of DNA or RNA into cells.
Visual acuity	Sharpness of central vision.

X
X-linked RP	A pattern of inheritance where female members of a family are carriers of RP. They have a 50% chance of producing a son with the disease and a 50% chance of having daughters who will be carriers.